WAGON
RECOGNITION

Martin Buck & Mark Rawlinson

⁂ **VTG**

Volume 1
Carkinds - B to W

FREIGHTMASTER

PUBLISHING

Compilation & Design : Martin Buck

Research : Mark Rawlinson

ISBN : 978-0-9558275-0-1

Published by : Freightmaster Publishing
158 Overbrook
SWINDON
SN3 6AY

www.freightmasterpublishing.co.uk

01793 - 644957

Printed by : Stephens & George Ltd
Goat Mill Road
Dowlais
MERTHYR TYDFIL
CF48 3TD

Cover design : Martin Buck

CONTENTS

March 2008

Opposite :

Class 60 No. 60072 *Cairn Toul* passes through Moreton Cutting, near Didcot, with 6B33, Theale - Robeston empty petroleum tanks, comprising a mix of TDA / TEA vehicles.   *(Martin Buck)*

INTRODUCTION

Welcome

to Wagon Recognition, Volume 1, the first all-inclusive colour guide illustrating the many wagon types, and their associated liveries, operating in revenue earning service on Britain's railways today. The perfect companion for enthusiasts, modellers and railway professionals alike.

Volume 2 will feature departmental wagons in the 'Y' and 'Z' Carkind categories plus plant and support vehicles.

How 'Wagon Recognition' came about

I was looking through a copy of *Freightmaster* and jotted down the terms used to describe some of the freight flows - MGR, bogie tanks, intermodal, for example, wondering if it would be possible to:

- establish how many different wagon types are in active revenue earning traffic, and,
- if individual freight flows can be identified by wagon type and livery, etc.

I decided to investigate further by observing freight traffic at close quarters and a visit was made to two local freight 'Hotspots' - Newport and Eastleigh - ideal for steel and intermodal traffic, respectively.

Steel traffic was particularly noteworthy with wagons of varying shapes and sizes: steel sided, canvas sided, bogie carriers, etc, not to mention European wagons registered to operate within the UK. In addition, there were other flows where the train was formed entirely of specific wagon types and livery, such as:

- blue enclosed car carriers (WIA's) conveying expensive cars from Washwood Heath to Southampton Eastern Docks for export.

- four types of '*Murco*' 100-tonne bogie tanks (TDA / TEA) in the consist of the Robeston - Theale petroleum tanks. (see page 2)

The subject matter was overwhelming, not to say incredibly interesting, leaving Mark Rawlinson and myself convinced a concise reference book, packed with colour photographs, illustrating wagon types and liveries, would be a good idea ....

.... '*Wagon Recognition*' was born!

I began familiarising myself with all the different wagon types and purchased a selection of wagon books, aimed really at 'number crunchers' - copious sequences of numbers, listed according to wagon ownership - 'Railway Owned', 'Privately Owned, 'Internationally Registered', etc.

Unfortunately, these books only led to more questions than answers;

- which wagon types are actually in revenue earning service and can be seen running on the main line?

- which are 'active' and which are stored or withdrawn?

- how do you identify one wagon type from another, especially if several share the same number range?

- which international (RIV) wagons operate in the UK?

Meanwhile, Mark set out to find some answers, doing his own research by analysing endless reams of TOPS lists and wagon fleet lists, resulting in an up-to-date list of the wagons operating in revenue earning service. These details form the basis of this book, which were initially made available through the *Freightmaster* 'OnLine' website for the benefit of subscription customers.

About this book

Firstly, this book **does not** include:

- lists of wagon numbers for 'number crunchers'.
- technical measurements.
- 'departmental' wagons (Prefix codes 'Y' and 'Z'),
- Plasser, plant and other associated vehicles.

It **does include:**

- wagon types in 'revenue earning' service.
- a photograph of the wagon, in its current livery(s).
- details of the 'active' number range of the wagons, complete with any prefix.
- details of trains / routes where the wagons may be seen in action.

Wagons are listed alphabetically according to 'Carkind' - a three letter code, which identifies the type:

BAA	Bogie Steel Wagon
to	
WIA	Articulated Car Carrier

There are over 200 Carkind listings in this book, supported by some 300 images to illustrate the various types and associated liveries. So, if you want to know what a *Freightliner Heavy Haul* JGA bogie aggregate hopper in the FLHH 17302 - 17324 number range looks like and where to see them running - this book is for you!

During compilation, several Carkinds were taken out of revenue earning service and, whilst excluded from the main part of the book, are recorded in the Glossary for completeness.

Finally,

Acknowledgements ....

I would like to thank VTG Rail UK Ltd for supporting this project along with all the people named on page 222 who have kindly contributed images. However, particular thanks go to Gareth Bayer and Martyn Read, whose websites on rolling stock have been an invaluable source of information.

So, whatever your interest, please now enjoy 'WAGON RECOGNITION'.

Martin Buck
March 2008

VTG Rail UK Ltd.

VTG Rail UK Ltd is part of VTG AG, who from its headquarters in Hamburg, Germany, operates approximately 50,000 wagons throughout Europe and North America in addition to tank container logistics, freight forwarding and specialised train operations. As part of this group, VTG Rail UK has access to a wealth of experience and resources to further support its UK operations. The UK fleet numbers approximately 2,000 wagons with newly manufactured vehicles being added as part of a continuous renewal process.

VTG Rail UK sets itself the highest quality standards. Operating under a rigorous quality assurance system, overseen at Group level, the company monitors all aspects of performance relating to wagons and services in order to provide customers with the highest levels of safety and reliability for the transport of their goods.

Committed to remaining at the forefront of the rail freight wagon leasing market, VTG Rail UK has invested in extra bulk cargo wagons to meet the demand for transporting increasing amounts of solid material and was the first company to introduce aluminium, 102 tonne, bogie cement wagons into the UK. The wagon's innovative aluminium tank construction minimises tare weight, giving a dramatic improvement in carrying capacity and, fitted with 75 mph, track friendly bogies, the wagons are capable of operating cost effectively throughout the UK rail network.

For practicality and operational convenience, VTG's UK wagon fleet is divided into two distinct sectors. The Bulk fleet is primarily concerned with the transportation of dry and solid products, whilst the Tank fleet has specialist equipment used for the transportation of most liquid, chemical and compressed gas products.

Both fleet sectors demonstrate VTG's commitment to meeting customer requirements, with wagons tailored to interface with loading and unloading points to speed the flow of goods through distribution channels. VTG's ability to modify or purpose build vehicles as required is unsurpassed within the industry. A flexible approach and rapid response to the needs of the customer makes VTG the first choice partner for all your rail freight vehicle requirements.

Vehicle types currently available include:

- 2 and 4-axle tank wagons for Class A and B petroleum products, bitumen, liquefied gases including chemical gases, liquid chemicals (stainless and lined mild steel), and chemical slurries

- 2 and 4-axle hopper wagons for carrying aggregates, chemicals, grain and other granular and powdered materials

- 2 and 4-axle open and closed box wagons for use in aggregates, rail infrastructure projects, scrap steel and waste transportation.

- 4-axle steel coil carrying wagons

- Wagons for Intermodal operations, including the Advanced Container Transport System (ACTS), and wagons for carrying excavators to infrastructure sites.

VTG Rail UK can offer flexible leasing and hiring arrangements for short and long term contracts and arrange additional services such as wagon loading and discharge if required.

For more information contact: Ian Shaw - Sales Manager
01905 750903
email salesuk@vtg.com,
or visit www.vtg-rail.co.uk .

OVERVIEW

TOPS CODES

In 1973, British Rail introduced a numbering system known as TOPS (Total Operating Processing System) to manage the movement of both locomotives and freight rolling stock. Accordingly, whilst each wagon had a unique number, each type would be classified by way of a three letter TOPS coding, called a 'Carkind', whereby:-

The **First Letter** identifies the Wagon category.

B	Bogie Steel Carriers
C	2-Axle Covered Hoppers
F	2-Axle & Bogie Flat Wagons
H	2-Axle & Bogie Hoppers
I	Internationally Registered Vehicles
J	Bogie Wagons
K	Special Wagons
M	2-Axle & Bogie Mineral Wagons
O	2-Axle Open Wagons
P	2-Axle Wagons
R	Railway Operating Vehicles
S	2-Axle Steel Carriers
T	2-Axle & Bogie Petrochemical Tank Wagons
V	Vans
W	Articulated Car Carriers
Y	Bogie Departmental Wagons / Track Machines
Z	2-Axle Departmental Wagons

The **Second Letter** identifies the Wagon Type:

Wagon size / capacity, etc.

'I' is used for internationally numbered vehicles.

The **Third Letter** identifies the brake type:

A	Air Brake
B	Air Brake, through vacuum pipe
X	Dual Brake - air & vacuum Brake

In 1973, about 10% of revenue earning freight traffic employed air brake wagons, whereas today the figure is 100% and all newly built wagons are automatically fitted with air brakes. The wagon categories in this book are all Air Brake (A) with less than a dozen examples of wagons fitted with an Air Brake through a Vacuum Pipe (B) and none in the 'X' category.

So, the three letters of Carkind **OAA** represent:

O	2-Axle Open Wagon
A	Wagon size, capacity specification.
A	Air Brake

NUMBERING SYSTEMS

There are three methods of wagon numbering in use:

1. Privately Owned Wagons

(Numbered 3000 to 99999)

Wagons owned by railway customers and leasing companies are numbered in the four and five digit series, but to avoid 'clashing' with loco/coaching stock numbers, they also carry a prefix before the main number.

For example :

NLU 29297   (JNA : Bogie Ballast Wagon)

PR   70065   (TUA : Procor 2-Axle Fuel Oil Tank)

2. Railway Owned Wagons

(Numbered 100000 to 999999)

Wagons owned by railway operators are numbered in a six-digit series and include:

Direct Rail Services
English, Welsh & Scottish Railways
First GBRf
Freightliner
Jarvis / Fastline
Network Rail

For example :

100091   (OAA : EWS 2-Axle Open Wagon)

358492   (HAA : 2-Axle MGR Coal Hopper

643014   (FEA : Fastline Bogie Twin Intermodal Flat)

Images : Martin Buck

3. Internationally Registered Wagons

These can be privately or railway owned wagons, capable of moving between countries in the European Community (EEC), and must be numbered in the **RIV** (international standard) number system.

The following details apply to wagons *seen in traffic in the UK*.

For example : **33. 87. 7797. 011 - 6** (an ICA Bogie Tank) where,

33	=	the Exchange Code (privately owned bogie wagon, fixed gauge)
87	=	the Country Code (France, in the above example)
7797	=	the Wagon Type code
011	=	the Vehicle Number
6	=	a computer check digit

3a. RIV 'Exchange' Codes for wagons seen in traffic in the UK

21	=	2-Axle vehicle, railway owned
23	=	2-Axle vehicle, privately owned
24	=	2-Axle vehicle, privately owned (variable gauge)
31	=	Bogie vehicle, railway owned
33	=	Bogie vehicle, privately owned
43	=	2-Axle vehicle, privately owned*
81	=	Bogie vehicle, railway owned*
83	=	Bogie vehicle, privately owned*

> * these wagons are restricted to the country of origin, but can work through the Channel Tunnel by special arrangement.

3b. RIV 'Country' Codes

68	=	Ahaus Alstatter Eisenbahn (AAE - German leasing Co.)
70	=	UK
71	=	Spain
80	=	Germany
83	=	Italy
87	=	France

3c. RIV 'Wagon Types'

2xxx	=	Vans*
4xxx	=	Intermodal flats, car carriers and steel wagons
6xxx	=	Hoppers
7xxx	=	Tanks
9xxx	=	Special vehicles : Covered Hoppers
0xxx	=	Special vehicles : Covered Hoppers, plus some steel carriers

> * some bogie vans are numbered in the 4xxx range.

3c. RIV 'Vehicle Number'

The digits 9 - 11 are the vehicle number.

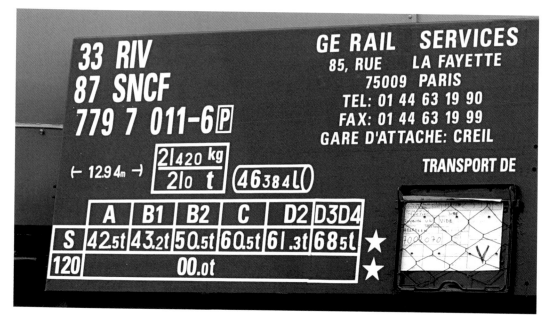

(Jim Ramsay)

3d. RIV Computer Check Digit

The 12th digit in the RIV number is a computer check digit, calculated by reference to the other 11 digits of the RIV number. The individual digits are multiplied alternately by 2 and 1 with the resultant numbers added together to arrive at the 12th digit.

For example using 33. 87. 7797. 011 the 12th digit will be calculated as follows:

Number	Multiplied By	Equals
3	2	6
3	1	3
8	2	16*
7	1	7
7	2	14*
7	1	7
9	2	18*
7	1	7
0	2	0
1	1	1
1	2	2

* Any number greater than 9 is taken as the sum of the individual digits.

Therefore, 6 + 3 + 1 + 6 + 7 + 1 + 4 + 7 + 1 + 8 + 7 + 0 + 1 + 2 = 54.

The sum is then subtracted from the next multiple of 10 above the sum reference.

So, 60 - 54 = **6**

(Martyn Read)

RIV Renumbering & Recoding

During their working life, many internationally registered vehicles such as KVA (EWS Cargowaggon) or FIA (EWS Multifret) are transferred from one country to another. As well as gaining a "70" country code, those which are bought by operators in the UK also change carkind from Ixx to a 'domestic' carkind such as KVA or FIA.

For example: The above illustration depicts ....

IFA (33) 87. 4908. 673 - 6

which is an intermodal flat at Washwood Heath, Birmingham, having arrived with 'Norfolk Line' swapbodies on the 6X82 automotive service from Wembley .

However, this vehicle has since been recoded, becoming ....

FIA (31) 70. 4908. 673 - 6

This can be confusing and over a given period, some railway enthusiasts can be forgiven in believing that these are two different wagons, when they are actually one of the same, albeit with a new number!

So, beware of this idiosyncrasy in what is a rather bizarre numbering scheme!

Opposite :

Under an almost solid canopy of electrification catenary, Class 66/5 No. 66512 approaches Rugeley Trent Valley station with a rake of JNAs loaded with ballast, running as 6G16, Stud Farm - Crewe Basford Hall.

(Martin Buck)

LEGEND

For each 'Carkind' listed, the following details are given:

1. 3-Letter 'Carkind' reference.
2. Wagon title.
3. 'Active' Number Range in which the wagon(s) will be listed.
   Reference is also made to wagons sharing a number range with another Carkind.
4. Notes (where applicable) of any important details, such as conversions, etc.
5. Freight Flows the wagons can be found working in revenue earning traffic:

    'Specific' Flows   :   Flows the wagons <u>only</u> work.

    'Typical' Flows   :   Examples of flows where the wagons can be found working, sometimes in conjunction with other wagon types.

    'Flows'   :   General flows across the UK, such as infrastructure trains, etc.

Example:

BCA   Bogie Steel Coil Wagon

Number range

900011 - 900304   (Numbered within BBA 900 series)

Notes

The BCA wagon is an open bogie coil carrier converted from surplus BAA and BBA steel flats.

Specific flows

Steel Coil :   Port Talbot and Llanwern to Trostre / Corby / Hartlepool

---

Each separate Carkind listing is backed up by an illustration to show the design and any associated livery(s), plus an informative caption providing details of the:

     - Carkind reference
     - Vehicle number
     - Location of illustration
     - Manufacturer(s) details for the Carkind
     - Photograph accreditation

Opposite :

Class 66/0 No. 66026 passes the site of Frodingham depot, Scunthorpe, with a rake of KFA flats conveying Greater Manchester Council domestic waste containers, forming 6M07 10:33 Roxby - Pendleton empty 'Binliner'.

In the background are some loaded EWS HTA coal hoppers working the Immingham - Scunthorpe steelworks circuit and an assortment of BEA bogie bolster wagons and a solitary BAA bogie steel wagon No. 900061.

(Martin Buck)

Carkind
Alphabet

BAA   Bogie Steel Wagon

Number range

900000 - 900305

BBA   Bogie Steel Wagon

Number range

910001 - 910590

Notes

These are the standard open bogie steel design. Over the years, many BAAs and BBAs have been converted to coil carriers and recoded BCA / BLA / BXA / BZA but still retain their BAA numbers.

The BBA is a 'stretched' version of the BAA; some converted to BSAs.

Specific flows

Steel Slab : Port Talbot to Llanwern

             Scunthorpe / Lackenby to Skinningrove / Dalzell

             Aldwarke to Deepcar

BCA   Bogie Steel Coil Wagon

Number range

900011 - 900304   (Numbered within BBA 900 series)

Notes

The BCA wagon is an open bogie coil carrier converted from surplus BAA and BBA steel flats.

Illustration, page 18.

Specific flows

Steel Coil : Port Talbot and Llanwern to Trostre / Corby / Hartlepool

BDA / BEA / BFA   Bogie Bolster Steel Wagon

Number range

950001 - 951249

Notes

Open bogie steel design with metal '*bolsters*' to keep the load in place; BFAs are also used as barrier wagons on pipe traffic to Laurencekirk. Illustrations, page 18 and 19.

Typical flows

Aluminium ingots :	Fort William and Lynemouth to Newport
Steel Sections :	Lackenby and Scunthorpe to Bristol
Steel Bar :	Scunthorpe to Brierley Hill
	Chatham Docks to Brierley Hill (via *Enterprise*)
	Cardiff Tidal to Rotherham
	Skinningrove to Tees Yard
Steel Plate :	Scunthorpe to Hartlepool

BAA
No. 900128

Built : 1972 - 1976 by BREL Ashford / Shildon
Location : Newport

(Martin Buck)

BBA
No. 910008

Built : 1973 - 1981 by BREL Ashford
Location : Cardiff Central

(Martin Buck)

BCA
No. 900094

Built   : 1972 - 1976 by BREL Ashford / Shildon
Location : Newport

(Martin Buck)

BDA
No. 950198

Built   : 1975 - 1981 by BREL Ashford / Shildon
Location : Rugby

(Martin Buck)

BEA	**Built**	: 1975 - 1981 by BREL Ashford / Shildon
No. 950697	**Location**	: Tees Yard

(Martin Buck)

BFA	**Built**	: 1975 - 1981 by BREL Ashford / Shildon
No. 950249	**Location**	: Tees Yard

(Richard Jones)

BIA	**Bogie Steel Wagon**

Number range : 910024 - 910535   (Numbered within BBA 910 series)

Notes : The BIA is a covered steel carrier with a sliding roof, fitted with five cradles. Converted from surplus BBAs.

Identical from the outside to BWA and BXA - illustration, page 22.

Typical flows : Steel - Immingham to Wolverhampton

BLA	**Bogie Steel Coil Wagon**

Number range : 910005 - 910588   (Numbered within BBA 910 series)

Notes : The BLA is a 'stretched' version of a BCA, numbered within the BBA number series.

Illustration, page 23.

Specific flows : Steel Coil - Port Talbot and Llanwern to Corby / Hartlepool / Trostre

BMA / BNA / BPA	**Bogie Steel Plate Wagon**

Number range : 950025 - 951160   (BMA)   (Numbered within BDA 950 series)
965000 - 965014   (BPA)
965026 - 965077   (BMA / BNA)

Notes : Open bogie steel design with metal 'bolsters' to keep the load in place.

Typical flows : Same flows as BDA / BEA / BFA :

Aluminium ingots / Steel Sections / Steel Bar / Steel Plate

BMA	**Built** : 1980 - 1981 by BREL Shildon	
No. 950141	**Location** : Scunthorpe Steelworks	*(Andy Jupe)*

BNA
No. 965077

Built : 1980 - 1981 by BREL Shildon
Location : Tees Yard

(Martin Buck)

BPA
No. 965004

Built : 1980 - 1981 by BREL Shildon
Location : Toton

(Gareth Bayer)

BIA   Built : 1973 - 1981 by BREL Ashford   No. 910239   Swindon

(Martin Buck)

BLA   Built : 1973 - 1981 by BREL Ashford   No. 910253   Newport   *(Martin Buck)*

BRA   Covered Steel Slab Wagon

Number range

964001 - 964050

Notes

'Telescopic' steel carrying wagon with sliding roof. Numerous faults plagued its introduction, and many have spent most of their lives relegated to the status of 'barrier' wagons for the movement of buckeye fitted stock! BRAs and BYAs are identical in external appearance. Illustration, page 26.

Typical flows

Steel :   Llanwern and Port Talbot to Dee Marsh   / Round Oak / Teesside / Wolverhampton
        Hoo Junction / Immingham to Wolverhampton

BSA   Bogie Steel Slab Wagon

Number range

910001 - 910591   (Numbered within BBA 910 series)

Notes

The BSA wagon is a converted BBA, for use on the Immingham to Tinsley circuit, but reverted back to general slab traffic. Most are now in store. Illustration, page 26.

Specific flows

Steel Slab   :   Port Talbot to Llanwern
          Lackenby to Dalzell

BTA   Bogie Bolster Pipe Wagon

Number range

950187 - 950984   (Numbered within BDA 950 series)

Notes

Converted from BDA bogie bolsters. Illustration, page 27.

Specific flows

Pipe traffic :   Hartlepool to Laurencekirk   (via *Enterprise*)

BVA   Bogie Steel Flat Wagon

Number range

952001 - 952031

Notes

The steel is loaded on 'cassettes' which can be quickly loaded/unloaded. Illustration, page 27.

Specific flows

Steel : 'Steelbridge' traffic from Tinsley to Immingham

BWA   Bogie Steel Wagon

Number range

910234 - 910489   (Numbered within BBA 910 series)

Notes

Covered steel carrier with sliding roof, fitted with cradle, but 'eye to side.'

Converted from surplus BBA open wagons.

Identical from the outside to BIA and BXA - illustration, page 28.

Typical flows

Steel : Immingham to Wolverhampton

BXA   Bogie Steel Wagon

Number range

910112 - 910487   (Numbered within BBA 910 series)

Notes

Covered steel carrier with sliding roof, fitted with seven cradles.

Converted from surplus BBA open wagons.

Identical from the outside to BIA and BWA - illustration, page 28.

Typical flows

Steel : Immingham to Wolverhampton

BYA   Bogie Coil Carrier

Number range

966001 - 966260

Notes

'Telescopic' steel coil carrier fitted with a cradle (eye to side) and a slidng roof - illustration, page 29.

Typical flows

Steel : Llanwern and Port Talbot to Dee Marsh / Round Oak / Teesside / Wolverhampton
       Hoo Junction / Immingham to Wolverhampton

BZA   Bogie Steel Coil Wagon

Number range

900001 - 900290   (Numbered within BAA 900 series)

Notes

Converted from surplus BAA / BBA steel flats, fitted with a cradle - illustration, page 29.

Specific flows

Steel Coil : Llanwern and Port Talbot to Corby / Hartlepool / Trostre

BRA
No. 964015

Built   : 1999 by Thrall, York
Location : Newport

(Martin Buck)

BSA
No. 910387

Built   : 1973 - 1981 by BREL Ashford
Location : Clay Cross

(Graham Lee)

| BTA | Built | : 1975 - 1981 by BREL Ashford / Shildon | |
| No. 950586 | Location | : Tees Yard | *(Martin Buck)* |

| BVA | Built | : 2001 - 2002 by Kokuma, Sweden | |
| No. 952005 | Location | : Tinsley | *(Mike Honeyman)* |

BWA   Built   : 1973 - 1981 by BREL Ashford
No. 910440   Location : Doncaster   *(Martyn Read)*

BXA   Built   : 1973 - 1981 by BREL Ashford
No. 910264   Location : Swindon   *(Martin Buck)*

BYA
No. 966073

Built : 1998 by Thrall, York
Location : Rugby Carriage Sidings

(Martin Buck)

BZA
No. 900084

Built : 1972 - 1976 by BREL Ashford / Shildon
Location : Thornaby

(Martin Buck)

CBA   2-Axle Covered Limestone Hopper

Number range

362150 - 362199

Notes

Four wheel (ex-PBA) covered hopper, known locally as a 'White lady'.

Specific flows

Limestone :   Hardendale Quarry to Lackenby
                  Shap Quarry to Redcar

CDA   2-Axle Covered China Clay Hopper

Number range

375001 - 375123

Notes

Similar to HAA coal hoppers, the first 120 were built new in 1987, replacing vacuum braked wooden body clay hoods. Some additional wagons have since been converted from HAA coal hoppers.

One odd 'spotting feature' is that these wagons are different both sides and both ends, only one side features the slots in the side that allow rainwater to escape, this makes that side of the wagon more obviously weathered than the other. A winder for the retractable sheet is found on one corner of the wagon and these wagons are usually all the same way round in a train!

Specific flows

China Clay :   Various loading points to Fowey Docks

CDA	Built : 1987 - 1989 by BREL / RFS Doncaster	
No. 375122	Location : Middleway Crossing, St.Blazey	*(Martyn Read)*

CBA   Built : 1975 by BREL Ashford   No. 362162   Thornaby   (Martin Buck)

FAA   Built : 1999 by Thrall, York   No. 609096   Eastleigh

(Martin Buck)

FAA   *EWS* Bogie Well Container Wagon

Number range : 609001 - 609100

Notes : Standalone wagon.

Flows : Domestic intermodal services.

FBA   *EWS* Gypsum Flat Wagon

Number range : 600000 - 600023

Specific flows : Gypsum - Drax to Newbiggin / Hotchley Hill

FCA   *EWS* 2-Unit Flat Wagon

Number range : 610001 - 610400

Notes : EWS ordered 400 'standard' container flats, many employed on 'binliner' traffic, with each unit semi-coupled in pairs. Illustrations, page 34 and 35.

Typical flows : Domestic Waste - Refuse Transfer Stations to landfill sites

           Lime   - Containerised Lime from Thrislington to Margam

           MoD Traffic - MoD vehicles / stores within the UK, usually via *Enterprise*

           Steel   - Custom built coil carrying containers, mounted on intermodal flats working from South Wales to:

                       Dee Marsh / Round Oak / Teesside / Wolverhampton

FDA   *EWS* Twin Container Flat

Number range : 621454 - 621542

Flows : Infrastructure Operations   Illustration, page 35.

FBA   Built   : 1994 by Rautaruukki, Finland
No. 600023   Location   : Toton Junction   *(Richard Jones)*

FCA with containerised Lime
No. Not Known   Location   : Tees Yard   *(Martin Buck)*

FCA with containerised Steel
No. Not Known   Location   : Newport, Alexandra Dock Junction   *(Martin Buck)*

FCA   Built   :   2000 by Thrall, York
No. 610331   Location   :   Didcot

(Martin Buck)

FDA   Built   :   1967 - 1971 by BREL Ashford
No. 621499   Location   :   Tame Bridge

(Martyn Read)

FEA　60ft. 'Twin' Bogie Container Flat Wagon

FEA　60ft. Bogie Flat Wagon

Number range / Specific flows	**GBRf Intermodals**

630001 - 630044　FEA - A　(Twin)
640601 - 640630　FEA - B　(Twin)
650001 - 650054　FEA - C　(Twin)

Intermodal ：Felixstowe to Hams Hall / Selby / Doncaster
Gypsum　　：West Burton / Cottam to Hotchley Hill / Newbiggin

Number range / Specific flows	**GBRf Infrastructure**

640631 - 640693　FEA - S　　Infrastructure Services - fitted with 'Salmon' or 'Tench' modules.

640901 - 640922　FEA - S　　Metronet infrastructure services, intermodal services during the week.

Number range / Specific flows	**Freightliner Intermodal**

640001 - 640500　FEA - B　(Twin)
640701 - 640734　FEA - B　(Twin)

Intermodal services ('Freightliners') from UK ports to inland terminals

Nos. 640137 / 138 / 151 / 152 are on permanent loan to Freightliner Heavy Haul for use on the London area (Cricklewood and Dagenham) 'Binliner' services.

Number range / Specific flows	**Balfour Beatty**

640501 - 640514　FEA - B　　Infrastructure services
640571 - 640576　FEA - D　　NTC2 Track Construction Machine

Number range / Specific flows	**Transplant**

640931 - 640943　FEA - S 'Slingers'　　Infrastructure services - conveying rails / sleepers, Metronet engineering work.

Number range / Specific flows	**Freightliner Heavy Haul**

641001 - 641066　FEA - E　　Infrastructure services - conveying rails / sleepers

Number range / Specific flows	**Network Rail**

642001 - 642050　FEA - S　　'Water Cannon' trains during the Autumn 'leaf fall season'

Number range / Specific flows	**Jarvis Fastline**

643001 - 643024　FEA - B　(Twin)　　Intermodal ：Thamesport to Birch Coppice / Doncaster Trafford Park

(Illustrations, pages 37 to 42)

FEA - A	Built	: 2003 by Marcroft
No. 630003	Location	: Peterborough

(Gareth Bayer)

FEA - B	Built	: 2004 by Wagony Swidnica, Poland
No. 640626	Location	: Rugby

(Martin Buck)

FEA - B   Built   : 2003 - 2004 by Wagony Swidnica, Poland
No. 640006   Location   : Eastleigh   *(Martin Buck)*

FEA - S   Built   : 2004 by Wagony Swidnica, Poland
No. 640679   Location   : Parkeston Quay, Harwich   *(Martin Buck)*

FEA - C   Built   : 2003 - 2004 by Wagony Swidnica, Poland
No. 650043   Location   : Rugby   *(Martin Buck)*

FEA - S   Built : 2006 by Wagony Swidnica, Poland   No. 640912   Finedon Road, Wellingborough   *(Gareth Bayer)*

| FEA - B | Built | : 2003 - 2004 by Wagony Swidnica, Poland | |
| No. 640514 | Location | : Peterborough Crescent WRD | *(Gareth Bayer)* |

(Top Right) :

| FEA - S | Built | : 2007 by Wagony Swidnica, Poland | |
| No. 640931 | Location | : Finedon Road, Wellingborough | *(Gareth Bayer)* |

(Bottom Right) :

| FEA - E | Built | : 2004 - 2005 by Wagony Swidnica, Poland | |
| No. 641021 | Location | : Washwood Heath, Birmingham | *(Martin Buck)* |

| FEA - D | Built | : 2004 by Wagony Swidnica, Poland | |
| No. 640572 | Location | : March | *(Gareth Bayer)* |

FEA - F   Built   : 2005 by Trinity Rail Group, Romania
No. 642015   Location : Didcot   *(Martin Buck)*

FEA - B   Built   : 2006 by Wagony Swidnica, Poland
No. 643002   Location : Rugby   *(Martin Buck)*

FIA   *EWS* "Megafret" Intermodal Twin Container Flat

Number range

31. 70. 4908. 654 to 749   31. 70. 4938. 000 to 224   33. 70. 4938. 300 to 743

Notes

FIAs are bar-coupled, but regarded as one wagon and so they share one number which is carried by the left-most platform.

Some FIAs are fitted with a frame to carry steel. Illustrations, page 44.

Flows

Intermodal   : Domestic services
                       European services via Channel Tunnel

Steel   : Scunthorpe to Ebange, France.

FJA   *EWS* Bogie Flat Wagon

Number range

621900 - 621917

Notes

Built 1967 - 1971 by BREL Ashford / Converted 2002 by Marcroft. Illustration, page 45.

Flows

Infrastructure Operations

FKA   *EWS* Intermodal Twin Low Platform Flat

Number range

(81) 70. 4908. 000 to 149

Notes

The FKA is formed of two platforms, but both platforms are regarded as one wagon, so they share one number carried by the left-most platform. Illustration, page 46.

Flows

Domestic Intermodal services

FLA   *Freightliner* Twin Low Platform Container Flat

Number range

605001 - 605028 (Inners)   606001 - 606020 (Outers)   606101 - 606180 (Outers)

Notes

The 6050xx and 6060xx date from Railfreight Distribution days and are normally formed into sets of 4 or 5 wagons, whilst the 6061xx series are a newer build, with all outer wagons semi-permanently coupled in pairs. Illustrations, page 45 and page 47.

Flows

Container services between British ports and UK terminals

FIA
No. 33. 70. 4938 series

Built 　　: 1994 by Arbel Fauvet, France
Location : Eastleigh

(Martin Buck)

FIA - Steel Frame Fitted
No. 33. 70. 4938. 539 　　　Location 　: Ashford 　　　　　　　　*(Martyn Read)*

FJA
No. 621905

Built   : (see text)
Location : Millerhill

(Martyn Read)

FLA
Nos. 606016 / 605017 / 605019 / 606015

Built   : 1991 by Powell Duffryn
Location : Didcot East Junction

(Martin Buck)

FKA   Built : 1999 by Thrall, York   No. 81. 70. 4908. 134   Tees Yard   *(Martin Buck)*

FLA   Built : 1991 by Powell Duffryn   Nos. 606175 / 606176   Didcot Parkway   *(Martin Buck)*

FNA — *DRS* Flatrol Atomic Flask Wagon

Number range : 550009 - 550060

Notes : Several different manufacturers:

Nos. 550009 - 550014	1976 by BREL Ashford
Nos. 550015 - 550016	1978 by BREL Ashford
Nos. 550017 - 550018	1982 by BREL Shildon
Nos. 550020 - 550026	1986 by BREL Swindon
Nos. 550027 - 550060	1988 by Procor

Specific flows : Nuclear Waste - BNFL sites to Sellafield

FPA — 2-Axle Container Wagon

Number range : 400300 - 400343

Notes : Converted from PFAs (BGL 95334 - 95377) in 2002 by Marcroft.

Specific flows : Gypsum- Drax to Hotchley Hill

FRA — *FHH* Container Flat Wagon

Number range : 613001 - 613044

Specific flows : Containerised Domestic Waste - Bath / Cricklewood / Dagenham to Calvert.

FNA	Built	: (see text)	
Nos. 550058 and 550046	Location	: Ipswich	*(Martyn Read)*

FPA	Built	: (see text)	
No. 400315	Location	: Doncaster	*(Martin Buck)*

FRA	Built	: 2002 by Marcroft	
No. 613018	Location	: Swindon	*(Martin Buck)*

| FSA | Built | : | 1991 by Arbel Fauvet, France | |
| No. 608557 | Location | : | Eastleigh | *(Martin Buck)* |

| FTA | Built | : | 1991 by Arbel Fauvet, France | |
| No. 607113 | Location | : | Eastleigh | *(Martin Buck)* |

FSA   *Freightliner* 'Outer' Flat Wagon

Number range   : 608001 - 608560

Notes   : The FSA usually work as a pair of FSA wagons or a 4 car FSA / FTA set.

Flows   : Freightliner trains

FTA   *Freightliner* 'Inner' Flat Wagon

Number range   : 607001 - 607140

Flows   : Freightliner trains

FZA   Bogie Rail Wagon

Number range   : 600500 / 600501 / 600502

Notes   : No. 600500 was a prototype for a 'Salmon' replacement programme in the 1980s which never got the green light. It now runs semi-permanently coupled to RRAs No. 400001 and No. 110575, having previously been numbered YLA DB996699.

Flows

Infrastructure trains

FZA	Built	: Converted 2004 by RFS, Doncaster	
No. 600500	Location	: March	*(Gareth Bayer)*

HAA   2-Axle 'MGR' Coal Hopper

Number range

350145 - 359550   (Original range 350001 - 359550)

Notes

The most iconic 'modern' British wagon, designed to be capable of hauling coal in non-stop 'merry-go-round' trips between mines and power stations, and set up to be able to load and unload at slow speed without a need to stop the train.

With the design dating from the 1960's and a fleet size originally numbering in the thousands these wagons dominated coal traffic before the modern high capacity bogie wagons came into use. All surviving wagons became part of the EWS fleet on privatisation.

From the original HAA style coal hopper with automechanical discharge cabability, variant designs followed, thus:

Code	Description	Build Details
HAA	2-Axle MGR Style Coal Hopper	1964 - 1977 by BREL Ashford / Darlington / Shildon
HBA	2-Axle MGR Style Lime Hopper - with Canopy	1980 - 1982 by BREL Shildon
HCA	2-Axle MGR Style Lime Hopper - with Canopy	1964 - 1977 by BREL Ashford / Darlington / Shildon
HDA	2-Axle MGR Style Coal Hopper	1980 - 1982 by BREL Shildon
HFA	2-Axle MGR Style Lime Hopper - with Canopy	1964 - 1977 by BREL Ashford / Darlington / Shildon
HMA	2-Axle MGR Style Coal Hopper	1964 - 1977 by BREL Ashford / Darlington / Shildon
HNA	2-Axle MGR Style Coal Hopper - with Canopy	1964 - 1977 by BREL Ashford / Darlington / Shildon

Identifying individual types of wagon can sometimes be problematic as some of these wagons have had the middle TOPS code letter 'patched' several times.

Typical HAA flows

Coal :

New Cumnock to Earles Sidings (Hope Cement Works)

Parc Slip to Westbury Cement Works

Swansea to Immingham

Leith Docks to Cockenzie Power Station

Hunterston to Longannet Power Station

Newport Docks to Uskmouth Power Station

HAA
No. 355699

Built : (see text)
Location : Newport

(Martin Buck)

HAA
No. 358492

Built : (see text)
Location : Newport

(Martin Buck)

HBA   Built   : (see text)
No. 368378   Location : Tees Yard   *(Martin Buck)*

HBA   2-Axle 'MGR' Style Lime Hopper with Canopy

Number range

368378

Notes

This is a modified HDA wagon with a canopy.

Flows

Limestone :

Shap Quarry to Redcar

HCA   Built   : (see text)
No. 351077   Location : Thornaby   *(Martin Buck)*

HCA   2-Axle 'MGR' Style Lime Hopper with Canopy

Number range

351077 and 354295

(Numbers within HAA 350 series)

Notes

Modified HFA.

Specific flows

Limestone :

Hardendale Quarry to Lackenby and Redcar

Shap Quarry to Redcar

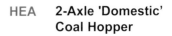

HEA   Built   : 1975 - 1979 by BREL Shildon
No. 360354   Location : Thornaby   *(Martin Buck)*

HEA   2-Axle 'Domestic' Coal Hopper

Number range

360002 - 361992

Notes

4-wheel hopper with gravity discharge, previously employed on industrial/domestic coal flows, but now confined to coke traffic.

Specific flows

Coke :

Redcar to Scunthorpe

HFA 2-Axle 'MGR' Style Lime Hopper with Canopy

Number range

353573 - 359292

(Numbers within HAA 350 series)

Notes

This is a standard/unmodified HAA with an aerodynamic canopy.

Specific flows

Limestone :
Shap Quarry to Redcar.

| HFA | Built | : (see text) | |
| No. 356957 | Location | : Tees Yard | (Martin Buck) |

HGA 2- Axle Ballast Hopper

Number range

390503 - 390670

Notes

These hoppers were converted from PGA stone hoppers by British Rail for engineers traffic, gaining the 'fishkind' *Gunnell* and TOPS code ZFA. On conversion, the wagon height was lowered and the length extended by adding triangular pieces to each end.

All these wagons are similar to each other, but due to being based on a wide range of older PGA hoppers there are lots of differences - height of body, smooth, part ribbed or fully ribbed bodies, for example, not to mention liveries!

During compilation, these wagons were replaced on stone flows originating out of Moreton on Lugg, Marks Tey and Stud Farm by new EWS HOA hoppers, but held as back up for infrastructure work in conjunction with the 2012 London Olympics.

Flows

Sand from Angerstein Wharf

| HGA | Converted : 1993 - 1994 by Marcroft | |
| No. 390575 | Location : Swindon | (Martin Buck) |

| HGA | Converted : 1993 - 1994 by Marcroft | |
| No. 390626 | Location : Swindon Transfer Sidings | (Martin Buck) |

HGA   Built : 1975 by Standard Wagon   No. 362094   Tees Yard   *(Martin Buck)*

HIA
No. 369093

Built : 2005 - 2006 by Wagony Swidnica, Poland
Wellingborough
(Martin Buck)

HHA   Built : 2003 - 2004 by Wagony Swidnica, Poland   No. 370436   Washwood Heath   *(Martin Buck)*

HTA   Built : 2001 - 2004 by Thrall, York   No. 310446   Washwood Heath   *(Martin Buck)*

HGA   2-Axle Lime Hopper

Number range

362000 - 362111

Specific flows

Limestone :

Hardendale / Shap Quarry to Lackenby / Redcar.   (Illustration, page 56)

HHA   *Freightliner Heavy Haul* Bogie Coal Hopper

Number range

370001 - 370446

Notes

Introduced by Freightliner Heavy Haul in 2000; built by Wagony Swidnica, Poland, with a carrying capacity of 73.6 tonnes and a top speed of 75mph. Illustration, page 58.

Flows

Power station coal traffic.

HIA   *Freightliner Heavy Haul* Bogie Limestone Hopper

Number range

(Green Livery)   369001 - 369021 and   369049 - 369122

(White Livery)   369022 - 369048

Notes

Separate number ranges, distinctive liveried hoppers, working individual limestone flows, although wagons will often interchange between flows. Illustrations, page 57 and opposite.

Typical flows

Limestone :   Dowlow to Barham / Kennett / Eggborough / Cottam
                Tunstead to Drax   / Ratcliffe / West Burton

Stone   :   Croft to Neasden

Sand   :   Wool to Neasden

HLA   EWS Bogie Aggregate Hopper

ex-Marcon

Number range   : 300702 - 300723

Notes

Ex-Marcon bogie hoppers now owned by EWS with some being renumbered from their previous numbers - MAR 17701 - MAR 17735 (old JHA numbers). Some retain their original livery.

Specific flows

Sand : Angerstein to Battersea / Luton Paddington / Park Royal / St.Pancras.

HLA   Built   : 1983 by W H Davis
No. 300709   Location : Ealing Broadway   *(Ian Delgado)*

HIA
No. 369043

Built   : 2005 - 2006 by Wagony Swidnica, Poland
Location : Doncaster

(Martin Buck)

HLA
No. 300720

Built   : 1983 by W H Davis
Location : Acton Mainline

(Martyn Read)

HMA
No. 350060

Built : (see HAA text)
Location : Newport

(Martin Buck)

HMA   2-Axle 'MGR' Coal Hopper

Number range

350010 - 359360
(Numbers within HAA 350 series)

Notes

The HMA is the same as an HAA, except it has a modified brake.

Flows

MGR coal services - as for HAA.

HNA
No. 356432

Built : (see HAA text)
Location : Thornaby

(Martin Buck)

HNA   2-Axle 'MGR' Coal Hopper

Number range

356432 / 357833 / 358745
(Numbers within HAA 350 series)

Notes

The HNA is a HMA with a canopy.

Illustrations of both canopied and non-canopied versions are shown, although the non-canopied vehicle is now in store.

Specific flows

Limestone :

Hardendale and Shap Quarry to Lackenby and Redcar

HNA
No. 356000

Built : (see HAA text)
Location : Newport

(Martin Buck)

HOA *EWS* Bogie Aggregate Hopper

Number range

320000 - 320067

(Right)	:	HOA
Built	:	2005 - 2006
		by Wagony Swidnica, Poland
No.	:	320053
Location	:	Cossington

(Martin Buck)

Notes

These wagons were introduced into traffic in 2007, to replace older aggregate wagons, especially the 2-axle HGA 'Gunnnell' wagons. Their first duties were the Middleton Towers - Ayr Harbour sand flow followed by stone workings from East Usk to West London. As more wagons come on stream, they will be found working other stone flows around the country.

Some hoppers carry Cemex colours (formerly RMC) and these will replace the older fleet of 89 orange coloured RMC (JGA) wagons, which will be deployed on other flows around the network.

Typical flows

Stone :

East Usk / Peak Forest / Stud Farm to various receiving terminals

Sand :

Middleton Towers to Mossend.

HOA	Built	: 2005 - 2006 by Wagony Swidnica, Poland
No. 320012	Location	: Great Rocks

(Martin Buck)

HQA   *Network Rail* Bogie Autoballaster

Number range

380001 - 380038 & 380501 - 380510	(HQA - A / D / G 'outers')
380101 - 380214 & 380601 - 380630	(HQA - B / E / H 'inners')
380301 - 380338 & 380401 - 380410	(HQA - C / F / J 'outers' with generator)
380701 - 380710	(GBRf Metronet HQA K / L / M)

Notes

The 'Autoballaster' is used by a number of companies and there is a range of corporate liveries:

> Network Rail

> Railtrack

> GBRf Metronet

Rather than duplicate images for each wagon type and livery, a selection of images are shown to illustrate the variations in livery.

A typical trainset comprises 5 wagons made up of 3 wagon types:

Outer wagon (with generator)

Inner wagon (without generator)

Outer wagon (without generator)

Flows

Ballast trains

HQA - J	**Built** : 2001 by RFS, Doncaster	
No. 380319	**Location** : Westbury	*(Martyn Read)*

HQA - D	Built	: 2004 by Wabtec, Doncaster	
No. 380502	Location	: Rugby	
			(Martyn Read)

HQA - L	Built	: 2006 by Wabtec, Doncaster	
No. 380707	Location	: Bedford	
			(Mark Franklin)

HTA   *EWS* Bogie Coal Hopper

Number range : 310000 - 311161

Notes

The HTA was introduced by EWS for use on MGR circuits around the UK, painted in the distinctive EWS red livery. These hoppers represent the largest order for one specific type of railway wagon since 1976, with each wagon capable of carrying 75 tonnes and running at 60mph loaded and 75mph empty. Illustration, page 59.

HTAs with the following numbers are fitted with buffers and have had 20,000 added to their number.

       330191 / 215 / 331 / 332 / 381 / 745

Flows   : Power station and industrial coal traffic.

HXA   *Freightliner Heavy Haul* Bogie Hopper

Number range : 370501 - 370719

Notes   : HXAs are a slightly shorter version of an HHA, but carry the same payload.

Flows   : Power station coal traffic.

HYA   *GBRf* Bogie Hopper

Number range : 371001 - 371072

Specific flows : Power station coal traffic - Tyne Dock to Drax
                                                 Hull Docks to Cottam
                                                 Welbeck and Thoresby to West Burton

HTA - Buffer Fitted No. 330332
No. 60056 on Fiddlers Ferry - Bescot HTA empties at Walton Old Junction, Warrington   *(Martin Buck)*

| HXA | Built | : 2006 by Wagony Swidnica, Poland |
| No. 370540 | Location | : Barnetby |

(Martin Buck)

| HYA | Built | : 2007 by IRS, Romania |
| No. 371012 | Location | : Knottingley |

(Martin Buck)

ICA   Bogie tank

Number range

(33) 87. 7797. 002 to 039

Specific flows

Calcium Carbonate :
Aberdeen to Irvine

Caustic Soda :
Runcorn to Dalry

ICA   Built   : 1989 by Arbel Fauvet, France
No. 33. 87. 7797. 018   Location : Carnoustie   *(Jim Ramsay)*

ICA / ICB   Bogie tank

China Clay traffic

Number range

(33) 87. 7898. 040 to 119

Notes

Built 1989 - 1990 and 2007 by Arbel Fauvet, France.

The 2007 build are specifically for a new Channel Tunnel flow from Belgium to Scotland, effectively replacing the long-running 6S55 flow from Burngullow.

Specific flows

China Clay Slurry :
Burngullow to Cliff Vale

ICA   Built   : (see text)
No. 33. 87. 7898. 119   Location : Par   *(Martyn Read)*   Antwerp to Irvine

ICA / ICB   Bogie Chemical Tank

Number range : (33. 80. 7794. 033 / 035   (ICA)
                    (33) 80. 7892. 004 / 009 / 010   (ICB)
                    (33) 80. 7894. 023 to 052   (ICB)

Specific flows : Chemicals (Chlorodifluoromethane) :
                      Ditton (ex-Runcorn) to Germany (Via *Enterprise*)

ICA   Bogie Caustic Soda Tank

Number range : (33) 87. 7994. 015 and 020

Specific flows : Caustic Soda :
                      Runcorn to Sellafield for use in the reprocessing of nuclear waste.

ICB	**Built**	: 1976 -1993 by Waggon Union, Germany
No. 33. 80. 7894. 028	**Location**	: Warrington Yard

(Martin Buck)

ICA	**Built**	: 1987 by A.N.F. Industrie, France
No. 33. 87. 7994. 015	**Location**	: Carnforth

(Tony Atkinson)

IFA   Built : 1967 by Frangeco, France   No. 23. 87. 4376. 012   Millbrook

(Martyn Read)

IFA — Car Carrier

Number range : (23) 87. 4376. 000 - 012

Notes : Flat wagons in 4-unit sets

Typical flows : Automotive -

Bordesley / Dagenham / Halewood / Portbury / Southampton / Tyne Dock
to & from
Dollands Moor / Garston / Mossend / Southampton

IFA / IFB — 4-Wheel Container Flat

Number range : IFA : (24) 71. 4438. 001 to 070 (French)

IFB : (21) 87. 4438. 000 to 448 (Spanish)

Notes : The IFAs work through to Spain as they are capable of changing gauge at the France / Spain border.

Illustration, page 72.

Specific flows : Automotive - Car component traffic from Dagenham to Silla, Spain.

IFA — *GBRf* Intermodal Flat

Number range : (33) 68. 4908. 102 to 209

Notes : Illustration, page 72.

Specific flows : Gypsum - Southampton to Mountfield (Containerised)

IFA — Long Welded Rail Wagon

Number range : (33) 83. 9314. 900 to 903

Notes : Illustration, page 73.

Specific flows : Welded Rails - Italy to Eastleigh

IFB — 2-Axle Steel Flat

Number range : (33) 87. 4145. 201 to 298

Notes : Illustration, page 73.

Specific flows : Steel Tube - France to Rotherham

IFA

No. 24. 71. 4438. xxx

Built : 1984 by Tafesa, Spain

Location : Stratford

(Gareth Bayer)

IFA

No. 33. 68. 4908. xxx

Built : 1990 - 2004 by Arbel Fauvet, France

Location : Lewisham

(Martyn Read)

IFA Built : 2002 by Costaferroviara Spa, Costamasnaga, Italy
33. 83. 9314. 900 Location : Clapham Junction

(S. Evans)

IFB Built : 1967 by Frangeco, France
No. 33. 87. 4145. 284 Location : Thornaby

(Peter Cummings)

IGA   No. 33. 80. 4647. 027   Carlisle   (Martyn Read)

IGA   No. 33. 80. 4736 series   Rugby   (Martin Buck)

IGB   No. 33. 80. 4742. 016   Scunthorpe   (Glenn Britcliffe)

IGA   Bogie Cargowaggon Flat

Number range   :   (33) 80. 4647. 000 to 049

Specific flows   :   Long Welded Rails - Workington Docks to Eastleigh

Number range   :   (33) 80. 4736. 000 to149

Notes   :   These IGAs originally conveyed imported steel to terminals such as Burton on Trent, followed (after conversion) operating Colas timber traffic flows between Carlisle and Chirk.

Specific flows   :   Long Welded Rails - Workington Docks to Eastleigh

Number range   :   (33) 80. 4742. 016 to 045   (All IGBs)

Notes / Flows   :   Four wagons in the number range used primarily to move switch gear and crossing components from France to Scunthorpe.

IGA Build Details :

Waggon Union, Germany

4647 series : 1983	4736 series : 1990	4742 series : 1979

IHA   Enclosed Steel Carrier

Number range

(33) 80. 4667. 000 to 049
(sliding roof)

(33) 87. 4667. 000 to 029
(canvas sided)

(31) 87. 4667. 043 to 099
(canvas sided)

(33) 87. 4767. 000 to 047
(canvas sided)

(31) 87. 4904. 000 to 060
(canvas sided)

Notes

These IHA covered steel wagons come in both a sliding roof and canvas-sided version with each type found in the UK, registered in France and Germany.

Illustrations, page 76 and 77.

Typical flows

Steel   :   South Wales to Burton on Trent / Dee Marsh / Round Oak / Wolverhampton

South Wales to France, via *Enterprise*

South Wales to Liverpool Gladstone Dock (via *Enterprise)*

Import traffic via 'Enterprise' to terminals such as Burton on Trent

Llanwern to Middlesbrough

IHA
No. 33. 80. 4667. 023

Built : 1985 by Linke Hofmann Busch, Germany
Location : Alexandra Dock Junction, Newport

(Martin Buck)

IHA
No. 33. 87. 4667. 025

Built : 1993 by Arbel Fauvet, France
Location : East Usk, Newport

(Martin Buck)

IHA

No. 33. 87. 4767. 005

Built   : 1982 - 1983 by Fauvet Girel, France

Location : Alexandra Dock Junction

(Martin Buck)

IHA

No. 31. 87. 4904. 012

Built   : 2001 - 2002 by Arbel Fauvet, France

Location : Newport

(Martin Buck)

IKA   Bogie 'Megafret' Intermodal Low Platform Flat (2-unit)

Notes

The IKA is formed of two platforms, but both platforms are regarded as one wagon so they share one number, which is carried by the left-most platform.

Some IKAs were fitted with a deck to carry vehicles - see illustration below.

Number range / Specific flows	EWS Intermodals
(31) 83. 4909. 200 to 299 / 500 to 684	Intermodal : Trafford Park to Dollands Moor
(33) 68. 4909. 312 to 518	Intermodal : Trafford Park to Dollands Moor

Number range / Specific flows	Freightliner Intermodal
(33) 68. 4943. 059, 69, 73, 74 and 90 to 99	Freightliners : Between Coatbridge and Seaforth

Number range / Specific flows   **DRS Intermodals**

(33) 68. 4909. 021 to 985

(33) 68. 4943. 060 to 088

Intermodal :   Daventry to Coatbridge / Grangemouth / Mossend
             Grangemouth to Aberdeen / Elderslie
             Newbiggin to Elderslie

IKA (4909 series) fitted with vehicle carrying deck   Location : Eastleigh   *(Martyn Read)*

IKA
No. 33. 68. 4909 series

Built : 1990 - 2004 by Arbel Fauvet, France
Location : Rugby

(Martin Buck)

IKA
No. 33. 68. 4943. 079

Built : 1990 - 2004 by Arbel Fauvet, France (converted 2004 - 2005)
Location : Rugby

(Martin Buck)

IMA   Italian Bogie Van

Number range

(31) 83. 2795. 001 to 200

Typical flows

Channel Tunnel Enterprise traffic.

INA   Articulated Bogie Twin

Number range

(34) 71. 4966. 001 - 002

Notes

Prototypes.

Nos. 4966. 001 & 002 awaiting certification to enter revenue earning service.

This is a three-bogied articulated flat that can take a pair of swapbodies, or be loaded with new road vehicles via drop down flaps.

Illustration, page 86.

Flows

Automotive

IMA	**Built** : 1984 - 1985 by Ferrosud & Officine, Spain	
No. 31. 83. 2795. 167	**Location** : Tavistock Junction, Plymouth	*(Allan Wright)*

IPA   Twin Single Deck Car Transporter

Number range : (43) 87. 4333. 001 - 081   (flats)

Notes   : 2-unit flat wagon

                Illustration, page 82.

Typical flows   : Automotive :

                Bordesley / Dagenham / Halewood / Portbury Dock / Southampton / Tyne Dock to & from Dollands Moor / Garston / Mossend / Southampton

IPA   4 Vehicle Double Deck Car Transporter

Number range : (23) 87. 4375. 002 - 050

Notes   : 4-Unit set.

                Illustration, page 82.

Typical flows   : Automotive - As for IPA 4333 series above.

IPA   4 Vehicle Twin Deck Car Transporter

Number range : (43) 87. 4384. 000 - 013   (4-unit sets)

Notes   : Build details : Nos 000 - 004 in 2004 by ABRF

                          Nos 005 - 013 in 2007 by SC Reva SA, Simeria, Romania.

                Illustrations, page 83 and page 84.

Typical flows   : Automotive - As for IPA 4333 series.

IPA   Twin Double Deck Car Transporter

Number range : (23) 87. 4392. 000 - 148 (2-unit sets)

Notes   : Illustration, page 83.

Specific flows : Automotive - Imported cars from Dollands Moor to Corby

IPA   Twin Double Deck Car Transporter

Number range : (23) 87. 4392. 500 - 745

Notes   : 2-unit sets

                Illustration, page 85.

Typical flows   : Automotive - As for IPA 4333 series.

IPA	Built	: 1982 by SNAV
No. 43. 87. 4333. 054	Location	: Eastleigh

(Martin Buck)

IPA	Built	: 1978 by Arbel Fauvet, France
No. 43. 87. 4375. 004	Location	: Washwood Heath

(Martyn Read)

IPA	Built	: (See text)	
No. 43. 87. 4384. 000	Location	: Washwood Heath	*(Martyn Read)*

IPA	Built	: 1983 by Duewag, Germany	
No. 23. 87. 4392. 100	Location	: Lewisham	*(Martyn Read)*

IPA   Built : (See text)   No. 23. 87. 4384. 007   Eastleigh   (Richard Jones)

IPA   Built : 1978 by Arbel Fauvet, France   No. 23. 87. 4392. 500   Washwood Heath   *(Martyn Read)*

INA   Built : 2005 by Arbel Fauvet, France   No. 31. 71. 4966. 002   Dollands Moor   (Barrie Swann)

IRB   Built : 1972 - 1974 by Arbel Fauvet, France   No. 33. 87. 0699. 004   Alexandra Dock Junction   *(Martin Buck)*

IRB   **Silica Sand Coverered Hopper**

Number range : (33) 87. 0699. 001 to 031

Notes   : 'Polybulk' design.

                       Illustration, page 87.

Specific flows : Silica Sand - France to Barry Docks (via *Enterprise*)

IVA   **2-Axle Cargowaggon**

Number range : (23) 80. 2398. 502 to 647   (23) 80. 2492. 001

Flows   : See IWA below for examples.

IWA / IWB   **Bogie Cargowaggon**

Number range

(33) 80. 2693. 000 to 050

(33) 80. 2797. 000 to 207   (33) 80. 2797. 508 to 633   (33) 80. 2797. 650 to 734

(33) 80. 2798. 000 to 014

(83) 80. 4741. 003 to 159

Notes

These are the 'standard' Cargowaggon van for many flows (domestic and Channel Tunnel). The Cargowaggons are pretty well identical and, as is the case with IWB, the design is the same, but built with a dual braking system. The 4741 series is distinctive in having a rounded roof.

Some wagons in the 2797 series are recoded KVA; see page 12 for explanation.

Illustrations, page 89 and 90.

Typical flows

Enterprise   : Channel Tunnel traffic serving terminals, such as Daventry.

Newsprint   : Immingham to Stanton Grove and Selby

                  Tilbury to Avonmouth

Paper   : Irvine to Daventry

Tinplate   : Trostre to Carlisle

Automotive   : Car components between Bridgend and Dagenham

IZA / IZB   **Cargowaggon, Twin**

Number range : (23) 80. 2928. 200 to 296   (23) 80. 2929. 000 to 199

Notes   : Some IZAs renumbered from 2929 to 2829 numbers.

                       Illustrations, page 91.

Flows   : See above.

IVA	Built	: 1983 by Duewag, Germany	
No. 23. 80. 2398. 642	Location	: Rugby	*(Martin Buck)*

IWA	Built	: 1988 - 1990 by Waggon Union, Germany	
No. 83. 80. 4741. 116	Location	: Rugby	*(Martin Buck)*

| IWA | Built | : 1985 by Linke Hofmann Busch, Germany | |
| No. 33. 80. 2693. 050 | Location | : Parkeston Quay, Harwich | *(Martin Buck)* |

| IWB | Built | : 1977 - 1978 by Linke Hofmann Busch, Germany | |
| No. 33. 80. 2797. 702 | Location | : Lostwithiel | *(Martyn Read)* |

IZA   **Built**   : 1986 by Duewag, Germany
No. 23. 80. 2929. 091   Location : Rugby   *(Martin Buck)*

IZA   **Built**   : 1986 by Duewag, Germany
No. 23. 80. 2929. 261   Location : Rugby   *(Martin Buck)*

JAA — Bogie Covered Lime Hopper — *Dowlow traffic*

Number range : VTG 13514 / 518 / 521 / 522

Specific flows : Lime - Dowlow to Mossend (via Enterprise)

JEA — Bogie Aggregate Hopper — *Brunner Mond*

Number range : BM 19701 - 19731

Specific flows : Limestone - Tunstead to Oakleigh (Northwich)

JFA — Bogie Aggregate Hopper — *Hanson*

Number range : ARC 17901

Notes / Flows : Prototype - see Page 106 (JHAs) for details and illustration.

JGA — Bogie Cement Tank Hopper — *Tunstead traffic*

Number range : BLI 11701 - 11730

Notes : This is a hopper-based tank design, hence the unusual JGA TOPS code

Specific flows : Cement - Tunstead to Leeds / Walsall / Willesden

JAA	Built	: 2000 by W H Davis	
No. VTG 13521	Location	: Peak Forest	*(Brian Daniels)*

| JEA | Built | : 2000 by W H Davis | |
| No. BLI 19704 | Location | : Peak Forest | *(Martin Buck)* |

| JGA | Built | : 2003 by Arbel Fauvet, France | |
| No. BLI 11717 | Location | : Peak Forest | *(Ian Delgado)* |

JGA   No. BHQ 17111   Acton Mainline   *(Martin Buck)*

JGA   No. BHQ 17140   Peterborough   *(Ian Delgado)*

JGA   No. AI 27101   Washwood Heath   *(Martyn Read)*

JGA   No. RMC 17235

JGA   No. RMC 13709

JGA   No. RMC 19235   *Illustrations (3) at Peak Forest by Martin Buck*

JGA Bogie Aggregate Hopper *Bardon*

Number range

BHQ 17101 - 17129 (Original design)   Built 1986 - 1988 by W H Davis

BHQ 17130 - 17151 (later build)   Built 1986 - 1988 by W H Davis

AI   27101 - 27122   Built 2005 by W H Davis

Notes

The AI series differ in design and livery with modern LTF bogies.

Illustrations, page 94.

Typical flows

Stone :

Bardon Hill to terminals, such as Angerstein / Brentford / Harlow Mill / Thorney Mill / Washwood Heath

JGA Bogie Aggregate Hopper *ex- RMC*

Number range

RMC 13700 - 13712   Built 1984 by Standard Wagon

RMC 17201 - 17249   Built 1986 by Standard Wagon

RMC 19220 - 19246   Built 1997 by Tatrastroj Poprad, Slovakia

Notes

A typical train set will normally comprise all three distinctive orange liveried hoppers in the number series listed above; some JGAs in the RMC17xxx series are similar in design to those in the RMC13xxx series.

Some hoppers in the 17xxx range display a PHA code!

Due to the Cemex / EWS contract signed in May 2007, some of the older RMC wagons were replaced by new EWS HOA hoppers (see page 63 for HOAs), with the JGAs passing to EWS for use on various stone flows in South East England; the 'RMC' logos obliterated from the sides of the wagons.

These wagons have become one of the most popular types of aggregate hopper amongst enthusiasts and so illustrations of pre and post Cemex vehicles are shown for comparative purposes.

Pre-Cemex illustrations, page 95.

Typical flows

Stone :

(Cemex) - Peak Forest to Bletchley / Ely / Salford Hope St. / Leeds / Selby / Washwood Heath.

(EWS)   - 'Common User' - Various stone flows around the country.

Opposite : **Post Cemex unbranded JGAs.**

These two illustrations show how the 'RMC' branding is being obliterated on wagons now finding work away from Peak Forest, such as this flow - 6V51, St. Pancras - Acton Yard.

Both photographs taken at Willesden Junction by Martyn Read.

(Top Right) : No. RMC 17240   *(Bottom Right) :* No. RMC 19132

JGA   Built : 1987 by W H Davis   No. FLHH 17312   Challow Station   *(Martin Buck)*

JGA   Built : 1991 by W H Davis   No. NACO 17453   Grangetown   *(Martin Buck)*

JGA	*FLHH* **Bogie Aggregate Hopper**	*ex- RH Roadstone*

Number range	: FLHH 17302 - 17324
Notes	: Nicknamed 'Jolly Green Giants'; illustration, page 98.
Typical flows	: Gritstone - Neath to Angerstein / Theale / Thorney Mill
	Stone - Wool to Neasden

JGA	**Bogie Covered Hopper**	*Boulby traffic*

Number range	: NACO 17450 - 17456 (former Cleveland Potash JGAs)
	NACO 19250 - 19280 (original Nacco salt JGAs)
Specific flows	: Potash - Boulby Mine to Tees Dock
	Rock Salt - Boulby Mine to Middlesbrough Goods

JGA	**Bogie Covered Hopper**	*Rylstone traffic*

Number range	: NACO 19170 - 19199
Specific flows	: Aggregate - Rylstone Quarry (nr. Skipton) to Hull / Leeds Hunslet / Redcar

JGA	**Bogie Covered Hopper**	*Hindlow traffic*

Number range	: BLI 19200 - 19219
Specific flows	: Limestone - Tunstead to Hindlow (Briggs Sidings)

JGA	**Built**	: 1998 by Arbel Fauvet, France	
No. NACO 19265	**Location**	: Grangetown	*(Martin Buck)*

JGA
No. BLI 19212

Built : 1994 by Tatratroj Poprad, Slovakia
Location : Great Rocks

(Martin Buck)

JGA
No. NACO 19199

Built : 1994 by Powell Duffryn, SA, France
Location : Gascoigne Wood

(Richard Jones)

JHA   Built : 1970 - 1971 by Chas Roberts   No. ELC 17517   Acton Mainline   *(Martin Buck)*

JHA   Built : 1989 by Orenstein & Koppel, Germany   No. OK 19364   Swindon

(Martin Buck)

JHA   Bogie Aggregate Hopper   *Brett*

Number range : ELC 17501 - 17520

Notes : A 'short & stubby' high capacity bogie hopper. Illustration, page 102.

Typical flows : Aggregate : Cliffe / Angerstein to Acton / Purley / St. Pancras

JHA   Bogie Aggregate Hopper   *ex-Marcon*

Number range : MAR 17701 - MAR 17733

Specific flows : Sand - Angerstein to Battersea / Luton / Paddington / Park Royal / St. Pancras.

JHA   Bogie Aggregate Hopper   *Yeoman*

Number range : OK 19300 - 19399

Notes : The first 20 wagons in the range are 'Outers' and the remainder 'Inners'.

Illustration, page 103.

Typical flows : Stone - Merehead to Botley / Eastleigh / Theale / Wootton Bassett

Jumbo train 'portions' to Acton / Brentford / Crawley

Sand - Grain to Theale

JHA   *EWS* Bogie Aggregate Hopper   *ex-National Power*

Number range : NP 19400 - 19420

Notes : Not to be confused with the ex-National Power JMA coal hoppers.

Typical flows : Stone - Whatley Quarry to St. Pancras

Tunstead to Bredbury / Pendleton (in mixed rakes with JMA hoppers)

JHA	Built	: 1969 by Chas Roberts / 1989 - 1990 by W H Davis	
No. MAR 17729	Location	: Hoo Junction	*(Ian Delgado)*

JHA
No. NP 19405

Built : 1993 - 1994 by Powell Duffryn Standard
Location : Stafford

(Martyn Read)

JHA
No. NP 19409

Built : 1993 - 1994 by Powell Duffryn Standard
Location : Westbury

(Richard Jones)

JHA	**Bogie Aggregate Hopper**	*Hanson*

Number range

ARC 17901 - 17932   (Outers)

ARC 19801 - 19912   (Inners)

Notes

These high capacity wagons were originally bought by ARC and wore their mustard livery, but have since gained Hanson colours.

This fleet is notable for the use of distinctive inside bearing TF1 low track force bogies. There are a few variants, the 17xxx's are outer wagons with buffers at one end and a buckeye coupler at the other, whilst the 19xxx's are inner wagons fitted only with buckeyes.

The Procor-built batch (19891 and higher) are a subtly different shape and the prototype ARC17901 (coded on TOPS as a JFA, but recorded as JHA on wagon bodyside) is different again.

Typical Flows

Stone :

Avonmouth/ Grain to Theale

Machen to Westbury

Mendip Rail 'Jumbo train' conveying portions for:

Allington / Ardlingly / Brentford / Dagenham / Hayes / Hothfield / Purley / West Drayton

JFA (Prototype)	**Built**	: 1990 by Bombardier Prorail	
No. ARC 17901	**Location**	: Hoo Junction	*(Martyn Read)*

Opposite : Photographs taken at Westbury by Martin Buck

JHA   No. ARC 17910   Built : 1990 by Procor and Standard Wagon

JHA   No. ARC 19892   Built : 1990 by Bombardier Prorail

JHA   No. ARC 19870   Built : 1990 - 1991 by Powell Duffryn Standard

JIA   Bogie Covered Hopper   *China Clay traffic*

Number range

(33) 70. 0894. 000 to 025 (Nacco)

Specific flows

China Clay :
Various loading points in Cornwall to Cliff Vale (Stoke) and Italy

JIA   Bogie Covered Hopper   *Boulby traffic*

Number range

(33) 70. 0894. 100 to 152

Specific flows

Potash :
Boulby Mine to Tees Dock

Rock Salt :
Boulby Mine to Middlesbrough Goods

JIA   Bogie Covered Hopper   *Dowlow traffic*

Number range

(33) 70. 9382. 004 / 010 / 029 / 030

Specific flows

Lime :
Dowlow to Mossend (via Enterprise)

JIA	Built	: 1974 - 1975 by Fauvet Girel, France	
No. 33. 70. 9382. 029	Location	: Peak Forest	*(Ian Delgado)*

JIA	Built	: 2001 by Arbel Fauvet, France
No. 33. 70. 0894. 017	Location	: Rugby

(Martin Buck)

JIA	Built	: 1997 by Arbel Fauvet, France
No. 33. 70. 0894. 125	Location	: Grangetown

(Martin Buck)

JJA	Built	: 2000 - 2001 by RFS Doncaster	
No. GERS **12903**	Location	: Bexley	*(Richard Jones)*

JJA	Built	: 2000 - 2001 by RFS Doncaster	
No. GERS **12926**	Location	: Westbury	*(Martyn Read)*

JJA — *Network Rail* Autoballaster

Number range	: GERS 12901-13005
Notes	: These rebuilt *Tiphook* KPA hoppers usually make up a 5 wagon train set, comprising 3 wagon types:
	Outer wagon (with generator)
	Inner wagon (without generator)
	Outer wagon (without generator)
	Some early numbered wagons still carry Carillion branding.
Flows	: Ballast trains

JMA — *EWS* Bogie Coal Hopper — *ex National Power*

Number range	: NP 19601 - NP19682
Notes	: Originally ordered by National Power - hence the blue livery - for use on MGR coal services to Drax, plus a twice-daily limestone train from Drax.
	Thereafter, coal traffic from Liverpool Bulk Terminal to Fiddlers Ferry, but due to frequent derailments, removed from these flows. There are currently two rakes in service working thus:-
Flows	: Stone - Tunstead to Bredbury / Pendleton
	Rylestone to Leeds

JMA	**Built**	: 1995 by OY Transtech, Finland
No. NP 19609	**Location**	: Peak Forest
		(Martin Buck)

JNA	Built	: (see text)	
No. VTG 3466	Location	: Acton Main Line	*(Martin Buck)*

JNA	Built	: (see text)	
No. VTG 3470	Location	: Westbury	*(Martin Buck)*

JNA   **Bogie Open Box Wagon**

Number range	: VTG 3162 / 3166 / 3167	built 1987 by Procor
	VTG 3400 - 3519	converted 1998 by Marcroft

Notes : A collection of wagons built for Mendip stone and Channel Tunnel construction traffic. Several design differences - access ladders, build style and bogies.

Some have conventional drawgear at both, one or neither end, the remainder having buckeyes!

Typical flows : Stone — various flows in south east England

Sand — Dagenham / Marks Tey to Colnbrook

GBRf Stone traffic — Stud Farm to Bury St. Edmunds / Marks Tey

JNA   **Bogie Box Wagon**   *Mendip Rail*

Number range : NACO 3900 - 3954   CAIB 3955 - 3989

Notes : The Mendip Rail branded wagon fleet is split between two leasers, CAIB and NACCO and are a mix of outers (buffers at one end, knuckle coupler at the other) and inners (knuckle couplers only).

Typical flows : Stone - Mendip quarry services (both direct trains and 'Portions') to receiving terminals, especially around London and the south east.

JNA	**Built**	: 2000 - 2001 by Marcroft
No. CAIB 3955	**Location**	: Westbury *(Martin Buck)*

JNA   Bogie Scrap Wagon

Number range : GERS 4400 - 4425   TIPH   9800 - 9835

Typical flows   : Scrap Metal - Handsworth / Kingsbury / Saltley to Cardiff Tidal
                               Willesden   / Snailwell to Sheerness

JNA   *Network Rail* Bogie Ballast Wagon   *'Falcon'*

Number range : NLU 29001- 29555

Notes   : A fleet of 555 Romanian built wagons used the length and breadth of the country.

Flows   : 'Virtual Quarry' ballast trains

JPA   Bogie Cement Tank Wagon   *Lafarge*

Number range : VTG 12401 - 12448

Notes   : New tank design introduced in 2007.

Typical flows   : Cement - Earles to Theale / West Thurrock

JRA   Bogie Aggregate Hopper   *Bardon, ex Camas*

Number range : (33) 70. 6905. 050 - 073

Notes   : These JRA's are unusually numbered in the RIV wagon series.

Specific flows : Stone - Croft to Bow

(Above) :

JPA	Built	: 2007 by VTG Feldbinder, Germany
No. VTG 12401	Location	: Doncaster *(Rob Terrace)*

(Bottom Left) :

JNA	Built	: 2003 - 2005 by Astro Vagone, Romania
No. NLU 29159	Location	: Eastleigh *(Martin Buck)*

(Below) :

JRA	Built	: 1988 - 1989 by Arbel Fauvet, France
No. 33. 70. 6905. 053	Location	: Harrowden Junction, Wellingborough *(Martin Buck)*

JNA   Built : 2002 by W H Davis   No. GERS 4402   Didcot   *(Martin Buck)*

JNA   Built : 1982 by Standard Wagon   No. TIPH 9831   Willesden Scrap Metal Terminal   *(Martin Buck)*

JSA   No. CAIB 3064   East Usk, Newport   *(Martin Buck)*

JSA   No. VTG 4131   Newport   *(Martin Buck)*

JSA   Enclosed Steel Carrier - Sliding Roof

Number range

CAIB 3063 - 3080	Converted in 1990s from JTA / JUAs built in 1972 by BSC Dorman Long.
VTG 4020 - 4134	Original JSAs built 1977 - 1978 by Dorman Long.
	Later examples (VTG 4100 onwards) converted in 2007 / 2008 by W H Davis, Langwith, from redundant JTA / JUA underframes.

Typical flows

Steel :

South Wales to Dee Marsh / Middlesbrough / Round Oak / Wolverhampton

JTA   Bogie Tippler - 'Outer'   *Iron Ore traffic*

Number range

BSSC 26097 - 26105

JUA   Bogie Tippler - 'Inner'

Number range

BSSC 26001 - 26094

Notes

These tipplers along with JUAs are used on the Immingham to Scunthorpe iron ore flow. They have rotary couplings enabling each wagon to be tipped over and the load deposited very quickly into a receiving shute. A typical train consist will comprise both JTA (outer) and JUA (inner) wagons.

Illustrations, page 120.

Specific flows

Iron Ore : Immingham to Scunthorpe

JTA   Bogie Tippler - 'Outer'   *Cliffe / Grain stone traffic*

Number range

VTG 26573 - 26740

JUA   Bogie Tippler - 'Inner'

Number range

VTG 26554 - 26841

Notes

Illustrations, page 121.

Typical flows

Sand	:	Cliffe to Battersea / Crawley
		Stud Farm to Crawley
Ballast	:	Grain to West Ruislip
Stone	:	Avonmouth / Stud Farm to Crawley

JTA	Built	: 1972 by BREL Shildon	
No. BSSC 26105	Location	: Barnetby	*(Martin Buck)*

JUA	Built	: 1972 BREL Shildon	
No. BSSC 26091	Location	: Barnetby	*(Martin Buck)*

JTA
No. VTG 26557

Built : 1972 - 1978 by Redpath Dorman Long
Location : Wandsworth Road

(Martyn Read)

JUA
No. VTG 26579

Built : 1972 - 1978 by Redpath Dorman Long
Location : Grain

(Martyn Read)

JXA   Bogie Scrap Wagon

Number range

PR   3000 - 3006   VTG   3100 - 3159

Notes

Former Sheerness (Co-Steel) scrap wagons, now owned by VTG.

Typical flows

Scrap Metal :   Hull / Mossend / Plymouth to Liverpool

JYA   Bogie Box Wagon   *Foster Yeoman*

Number range

OK 3268 - 3328

Notes

Built by Orenstein & Koppel in Germany, this is another wagon fleet that has a mix of outer (buffers one end, buckeye the other) and inner (buckeye only) examples.

These boxes are limited to 45mph to reduce track damage.

Typical flows

Stone   :   Merehead to Fareham

            Jumbo 'portions' to Colnbrook / Crawley

JZA   Bogie Long Welded Rail Carrier

Number range

NLU 93325 - 93463   (Numbered within KFA - TIPH 93292 - TIPH 93489 series)

Notes

Ex-KFAs.

Specific flows

Long Welded Rails - Scunthorpe to Crewe / Doncaster / Wellingborough

JZA   Bogie Long Welded Rail Flat Wagon

Number range

NLU 93600 - 93617

NLU 93700 - 93773

Specific flows

Long Welded Rails - Scunthorpe to Crewe / Doncaster / Wellingborough

JXA   Built   : 1974 - 1975 by Procor
No. PR 3000   Location : Warrington, Arpley   *(Martin Buck)*

JXA   Built   : 1972 - 1983 by Procor
No. VTG 3110   Location : Tavistock Junction, Plymouth   *(Martyn Read)*

JYA	**Built** : 1988 by C C Crump
No. OK 3308	**Location** : Swindon *(Martin Buck)*

JZA	**Built** : 1987 - 1988 by Rautarukki, Finland
No. NLU 93334	**Location** : Didcot Parkway *(Martin Buck)*

JZA   **Built** : 2002 by W H Davis
No. NLU 93617   **Location** : Didcot Parkway   *(Martin Buck)*

JZA   **Built** : 2002 - 2005 by W H Davis
No. NLU 93722   **Location** : Newport   *(Richard Jones)*

KEA   Bogie Box Wagon

Number range : PR 3170 - 3247 (being recoded VTG)

Notes : Similar to the JNA 39xx series, but different in terms of access ladders, build style and bogies. They come with conventional drawgear at both, one or neither end, the remainder having buckeyes!

Converted from redundant TEA bogie tanks, hence the KEA carkind!

At the time of going to press, only a handful of KEAs remain in traffic.

Typical flows : Stone - Merehead to Sevington / Stewarts Lane

KFA   Bogie Vehicle Transporter   *'Warflat'*

Number range : MODA 95233 - 95296

Specific flows : MoD Traffic

KFA   Bogie Open Sided Timber Carrier

Number range : GERS 97106 - 97309

Notes : Converted from former Cargowaggons; illustration, page 130.

Specific flows : Timber - Carlisle to Chirk

KFA   Electrification Module Carrier

Number range : WHD 97301 - WHD 97310

Specific flows : Infrastructure - electrification trains

KEA   Built : 1987 by Procor
No. VTG 31xx   Location : Westbury   *(Martyn Read)*

KFA
No. MODA 95282

Built   : 1976 - 1981 by BR Shildon
Location : Didcot Parkway

(Martin Buck)

KFA
No. WHD 97304

Built   : 2000 by W H Davis
Location : Tring

(Gareth Bayer)

KFA   Standard Container Flat

Number range / Flows

GMC	92500 - 92542	92580 - 92588	Roxby Binliner
RLS	92547 - 92562	92611 - 92651	Freightliner / MoD Traffic
AVON	92563 - 92579		Avon Binliner
TIPH	93292 - 93489		Freightliner / MoD Traffic
CAIB	95382 & 95385		Electrification Vehicles
EDC	95420 - 95431		Edinburgh Binliner

Notes

The KFA is a single flat with conventional buffers and drawgear at both ends - a basic unit on which 'containers' are transported for various commodities and organisations.

The KFAs in the RLS series can also carry custom built coil carrying containers working steel flows between South Wales and Dee Marsh / Round Oak / Teesside / Wolverhampton.

In some respects, whilst there maybe slight design differences between the individual number ranges, its not the 'flat' that provides the interest, but the payload - in particular, the uniform set of distinctive coloured containers which identify certain 'Binliners.' For example:

Binliner	*Colour of Containers*
Avon	Green
Greater Manchester	White & Yellow
City of Edinburgh	White

KFA	Built	: 1981 - 1985 by Remafer and Standard Wagon
No. GMC 92541	Location	: Healey Mills

(Martyn Read)

KFA
No. AVON 92564

Built : 1985 - 1986 by Powell Duffryn and Standard Wagon
Location : Swindon

(Martin Buck)

KFA
No. EDC 95420

Built : 1979 - 1982 by Procor
Location : Oxwellmains

(Martyn Read)

KFA   Converted 2007 by W H Davis   No. GERS 97138   Wrexham   *(Dave Skipsey)*

KJA   Built : 1989 by Standard Wagon   No. REDA 92635   Rugby   *(Martin Buck)*

KFA   Crane Match Wagon

Number range

GR 97401 - CN 97418 which include:

Balfour Beatty

BB 97403 / 404 / 410 / 411 / 412

Carillion

CN 97416 / 417 / 418

First Swietelsky

FS 97413 / 414 / 415

Grant Rail

GR 97401 / 402 / 405 / 406 / 407 / 408 / 409

Notes

A typical trainset comprises four vehicles, three of which are KFA support vehicles, housing equipment relating to the crane.

To avoid duplication, a Balfour Beatty KFA is illustrated.

Specific flows

Infrastructure services.

KFA			
No. BB 97403	Built	: 2001 - 2005 at York	
	Location	: Tonbridge	*(Richard Jones)*

KIA / KIB   Enclosed Steel Carrier

Number range : (33) 70. 0899. 000 to 104   (sliding roof)
              (33) 70. 4666. 000 to 054   (canvas sided)

Notes : Illustrations, page 134 and 135.

Typical flows : Steel :

South Wales to Burton on Trent / Dee Marsh / Round Oak / Wolverhampton
South Wales to France / Liverpool / Middlesbrough via *Enterprise*
Import traffic to Burton on Trent, via *Enterprise*

KJA   Self Discharge Bogie Unloading Wagon   *LaFarge*

Number range : REDA 92545 / 92546 / 92602 / 92635

Notes : This wagon is used in the Self Discharge train, which comprises four types of hopper wagons (see below) linked by an on-board conveyor belt, which feeds the discharge wagon (KJA) built from an old container flat. Illustration, page 131.

     PHA - P : Basic Hopper
     PHA - Q : Basic Hopper with Generator
     PHA - R : Basic Hopper fitted with belt tensioner
     PHA - S : Basic Hopper generator.

Specific flows : Stone : Used on Self-Discharge train - see under PHA on page 165 for details.

KRA   *Jarvis* Bogie Sleeper Carrier

Number range : NR 97101 - 97132

Flows : Infrastructure operations.   Illustration, page 136.

KSA   'Cube' Wagon

Number range : (33) 70. 4739. 001 to100

Notes : Originally built for conveying motor car panels from the Rover plant in Swindon to Longbridge. Surplus vehicles were then transferred for work on the DRS / W H Malcolm intermodals. Most are now in store.   Illustration, page 136.

Specific flows : Intermodal - W H Malcolm traffic from Grangemouth to Daventry.

KTA   *Freightliner* 'Pocket' Flat

Number range : GERS 97700 - 97774

Flows : Freightliner trains   Illustration, page 137.

KUA   Bogie Nuclear Flask Transporter

Number range : MODA 95770 & MODA 95771

Specific flows : 'Heavyweight' flask traffic to / from Sellafield.   Illustration, page 137.

KIA   Built : 1979 by Hofmann Busch, Germany   No. 33. 70. 0899. 093   Alexandra Dock Junction   *(Martin Buck)*

KIA   Built : 1987 - 1989 by Arbel Fauvet, France   No. 33. 70. 4666. 027   East Usk, Newport   *(Martin Buck)*

KRA   **Built**   :   1999 - 2000 by RFS Wabtec, Doncaster

No. NR 97108   **Location** :   Westbury   *(Martyn Read)*

KSA   **Built**   :   1995 by Arbel Fauvet, France

No. 33. 70. 4739. 098   **Location** :   Exeter Riverside Yard   *(Martin Buck)*

KTA   Built   : 1988 by Arbel Fauvet Douai, France
No. GERS 97731   Location : Didcot

(Martin Buck)

KUA   Built   : 1997 by Bombardier Prorail
No. MODA 95771   Location : Dawlish Warren

(Colin Marsden)

KVA   Bogie Ferryvan

Number range	: (83) 70. 2795. 300 to 349
	(33) 70. 2797. 102 to 311
Notes	: Illustration, page 140.
Typical flows	: Enterprise Traffic - To Cricklewood and Daventry

         Paper   - Irvine to Daventry

         Tinplate   - Trostre to Carlisle

KWA   Bogie Vehicle Transporter   *'Warwell'*

Number range	: MODA 95500 - 95583
Notes	: Built BREL Lancing & Ashford, 1942 - 1943 - refurbished 1980s.
	Illustration, Page 141.
Flows	: MoD Traffic

KWA   Bogie Excavator & Container Well Wagon

Number range	: CAIB 95610 - VTG 95639
Notes	: Two batches of 'excavator' wagons.
Flows	: Infrastructure operations.

KXA   Bogie Nuclear Flask Transporter

Number range	: BNFL 96901 - BNFL 96906
Notes	: Built late 2007 for British Nuclear Fuels, with two 4-wheel bogies at each end.
	Illustration on Page 142.
Specific flows	: 'Heavyweight' flask traffic to / from Sellafield.

KYA   Bogie Nuclear Flask Transporter

Number range	: (33) 70. 9986. 006 / 007 / 008
Specific flows	: Flask traffic to/from Sellafield.

KWA
No. CAIB 95614

Built : 2000 - 2004 by W H Davis
Location : Peterborough

(Gareth Bayer)

KYA
No. 33. 70. 9986. 008

Built : 1982 by BREL Ashford
Location : Sellafield

(Dave McAlone)

KVA   Built : 1985 - 1988 by Linke Hofmann Busch, Germany   No. 83. 70. 2795. 318   Rugby   *(Martin Buck)*

KWA   Built : ; (see text)   No. MODA 95510   Didcot   *(Martin Buck)*

MJA   Built : 2003 - 2004 by Wagony Swidnica, Poland   No. 502041   Swindon Transfer Sidings   *(Martin Buck)*

MBA   *EWS* 'Monster' Bogie Box Wagon

Number range

500001 - 500200

Notes

Built for EWS by Thrall Europa, these huge open boxes (hence the term 'Monster') are used for many different traffics.

The first 60 wagons are equipped with buffers and swinghead knuckle couplers, the remainder are fitted with only knuckle couplers.

EWS lowered the body height on a number of these wagons for infrastructure use and were recoded MCA and MDA on conversion.

These new wagons made history on 9/10 August 1999 when they were used on the first commercial freight to run on the privately owned North Yorkshire Moors Railway. Two trains conveyed scrap car metal for European Metal Recycling (EMR), brought by road from Malton, and ran via the 'Enterprise' sevice to Alexandra Dock, Liverpool.

Flows

Various flows around the country including:

Aggregate

Coal

Scrap Metal

Stone

Timber

MCA   Bogie Low Sided Open Box Wagon

Number range

500201 - 500240

MDA   Bogie Low Sided Open Box wagon

Number range

500241 - 500300

Notes

Converted from MBAs.

Flows

Engineers trains

(Top Right) :
MBA   Built   : 1999 by Thrall, York
No. 500184   Location : Peak Forest   *(Martin Buck)*

(Centre Right) :
MCA   Built   : 1999 by Thrall, York
No. 500202   Location : Bescot   *(Martyn Read)*

(Bottom Right) :
MDA   Built   : 1999 by Thrall, York
No. 500272   Location : Bescot   *(Martyn Read)*

MEA   No. 391032   Parkeston Quay

MEA   No. 391132   Parkeston Quay

MEA   No. 391473   Peak Forest

MEA   2-Axle Mineral Box Wagon

Number range

391002 - 391082
Converted : 1990 - 1993
by ABB Crewe & RFS Doncaster

391101 - 391160
Converted : 1995 by Toton C. & W.

391201 - 391698
Converted : 1996 - 2004
by Marcroft / Tees C. & W,
Barry Island / RFS Doncaster

Notes

These wagons were created by adding a box body onto a redundant HEA hopper chassis.

The earliest examples were converted by Trainload Coal, with Mainline Freight and Loadhaul also building batches. EWS continued to order batches to increase the fleet size.

The current fleet is mostly in EWS maroon livery, but many examples of Mainline Freight blue, Loadhaul black (no orange) and even a few Trainload coal ones are still in service.

Typical flows

Industrial Coal :
Immingham / Redcar / New Cumnock to:
Clitheroe / Ketton / Penyfford

Blending Coal :
Parc Slip to Onllwyn

Limestone :
Dowlow to Ashburys

All photographs (6) taken by Martin Buck

MFA 2-Axle Low Sided Open Box Wagon

Number range

391001 - 391617
(Same number range and conversion details as MEA)

Notes

These wagons were created by cutting down the sides of surplus MEA mineral boxes and, as with the MEAs, MFAs can be found in several 'obsolete' liveries.

Flows

Engineers trains :
randomly mixed with MHA and MTA.

MFA   No. 391131   Rugby

MHA 2-Axle Low Sided Open Box Wagon

Number range

394001 - 394400 Early body
394406 - 394410 Ex MAA*
394500 - 394999 Late body
396000 - 396165 Late body

Notes

These wagons were converted between 1997 - 2004 at RFS Doncaster by adding a box onto a redundant HAA (MGR) hopper and named Coalfish!.

* These are a small number of MHA wagons that were not rebodied but were cut down from MAAs (which had MEA-style bodies on an HAA chassis), similar in appearance to the early body Coalfish, but are slightly taller and wear a weathered trainload coal grey and yellow.

The 'Coalfish' branding is only carried by around 150 wagons in the early body style.

Flows

Engineers trains

MHA   No. 394544   Swindon Transfer Sidings

MHA   No. 394150   Rugby

MJA — *Freightliner* Bogie Box Wagon

Number range : 502001 - 502060 and 502200

Notes : These box wagons were built for Freightliner by Wagony Swidnica (Poland) during 2003, having buffers one end whilst the other is bar-coupled to the adjacent wagon, forming them into semi-permenant pairs.

Illustration, page 143.

Typical flows : Stone -

Various flows, including:

Dowlow to Garston / Ferrybridge

Mountsorrel to Luton
Croft to Harwich
Moreton on Lugg to Harlow Mill

MLA — Bogie Low Sided Open Ballast Wagon

GBRf / Metronet

Number range : 503001 - 503140

Notes : These distinctively coloured box wagons were built new for GBRf's ten-year contract with London Underground maintenance company Metronet.

Flows : Ballast workings.

Stone - Stud Farm to Bury St. Edmunds / Marks Tey.

EWS

Number range : 503501 - 503515

Notes : This is the first batch in an order of 105 new MLA wagons for EWS in 2008.

Flows : Ballast workings.

MOA — Bogie Low Sided Open Box Wagon

Number range : 500301 - 500350

Notes : A cut - down version of the huge MBA 'Monster Boxes' built for EWS by Thralll Europa and are buffer-fitted.

Flows : Engineers trains

MLA
No. Not Known

Built : 2008 by Wagony Swidnica, Poland
Location : Wagony Swidnica, Poland

(Courtesy EWS)

MOA
No. 500329

Built : 2003 by Thrall, Studenka Vagona, Czech Republic
Location : Bescot

(Martyn Read)

MLA   Built : 2006 by Wagony Swidnica, Poland   No. 503087   Acton Mainline   *(Martin Buck)*

MRA - B   Built : 2003 - 2004 by Astro Vagoane, Arad, Romania   No. 501090   Eastleigh   *(Martyn Read)*

MRA   Bogie Side Tipping Ballast Wagon

Number range

MRA - A :	501001 - 501060	Outer with Generator
MRA - B :	501061 - 501120	Outer
MRA - C :	501121 - 501300	Inner
MRA - D :	501301 - 501320	Outer
MRA - E :	501321 - 501340	Outer
MRA - F :	501341 - 501400	Inner

Notes

Side tipping ballast wagons, built between 2003 - 2004 by Astro Vagoane, Arad, Romania.

Wagons numbered 501301 onwards are in Network Rail Yellow. Network Rail has swapped a batch of these for a batch of new MLA box wagons built for the GBRF/Metronet contract, so some of the NR yellow examples are now remarked with Metronet logo's.

There are several designs within the range and to avoid repetition, four illustrations are included to reflect different designs and operators.

Flows

Ballast workings

All MRA photographs by Martyn Read.

MRA- A   No. 501051   Westbury

MRA- F   No. 501353   Tonbridge

MRA- F   No. 501350   Tonbridge

MTA 2-Axle Open Box Wagon

Number range : 395001 - 395405

Notes : These wagons were created by adding a box body onto the chassis of a redundant TTA tank wagon. Some wagons were converted from ZKA 'Limpets' and have slightly taller ends.

Flows : Engineers trains

| MTA | Converted : 1999 by RFS Doncaster | |
| No. 395090 | Location : Rugby | *(Martin Buck)* |

| MTA | Converted : 1999 by RFS Doncaster | |
| No. 395344 | Location : Newport | *(Martyn Read)* |

OAA	**2-Axle Open Wagon**	*Mendip 'Forticrete' traffic*

Number range : 100000 - 100099

Notes : There are many varieties of this type of wagon.

Specific flows : Concrete Blocks from Merehead to Acton.

OAA	Built	: 1971 by BREL Ashford	
No. 100088	Location	: Westbury	*(Martin Buck)*

OAA	Built	: 1971 by BREL Ashford	
No. 100010	Location	: Westbury	*(Martin Buck)*

OBA — 2-Axle Open Wagon

Number range : 110000 - 110800

Notes : There are many varieties of this type of wagon.

Flows : Engineers trains

| OBA | Built | : 1977 - 1979 by BREL Ashford / Shildon |
| No. 110000 | Location | : Didcot Yard |

(Martin Buck)

| OBA | Built | : 1971 by BREL Ashford |
| No. 110387 | Location | : Didcot Yard |

(Martin Buck)

OCA 2-Axle Open Wagon

Number range : 112000 -112398

Notes : Metal-sided version of the OBA

Flows : Engineers trains

| OCA | Built | : 1981 - 1982 by BREL Shildon | |
| No. 112240 | Location | : Didcot Yard | *(Martin Buck)* |

| OCA | Built | : 1981 - 1982 by BREL Shildon | |
| No. 112309 | Location | : Westbury | *(Martyn Read)* |

PAA   **2-Axle Sand Hopper**   *WBB Minerals*

Number range : WBB 30001 - 30060   WBB 30101 - 30112

Specific flows : Sand - Middleton Towers to Barnby Dun / Goole / Monk Bretton.

PAA   Built : 1981 - 1983 by W H Davis
Nos. WBB 30021 & WBB 30008   Location : Peterborough   *(Martin Buck)*

PAA   Built : 1981 - 1983 by W H Davis
No. WBB 30106   Location : Ely   *(Ian Delgado)*

PCA   2-Axle Cement Powder Tank

Number range

RC 10025 - 10049

Notes

The RMC logo will be blanked out under Cemex.

Specific flows

Lime Mortar Powder :
Peak Forest to Bletchley

PCA	Built	: (See text)	
No. 10025	Location	: Peak Forest	*(Martin Buck)*

PCA   2-Axle Cement Tank

Number range

BCC 10667 - 11141

Notes

These wagons come in a variety of shapes, including straight and depressed centre barrel designs, as illustrated on this page. There is also a third design, identical in build to the illustration shown top left, page 160, (save for the branding), which work the Oxwellmains circuit.

Typical flows

Cement :

Earles to Colnbrook / Dewsbury Moorswater / Seaham / Theale Weaste
Oxwellmains to Aberdeen / Ayr Inverness / Seaham Viewpark

PCA	Built	: (See text)	
No. 11019	Location	: Doncaster	*(Martin Buck)*

PCA Build Details:

Number range:

PR 10000 to BCC 11141

Built 1976 - 1987 by:

BREL
CFMF
Powell Duffryn
Procor
Standard Wagon

PCA	Built	: (See text)	
No. BCC 10771	Location	: Liskeard	*(Martyn Read)*

PCA	Built	: 1981 by CFPM
Nos. VTG10640	Location	: Harrowden Junction *(Martin Buck)*

PCA   2-Axle Cement Tank

Castle Cement

Number range

VTG 10600 - 10651

VTG 74030 - 74044

Specific flows

Cement :
Ketton to St.Pancras

PCA	Built	: (See text)
No. ALCN 11216	Location	: North Blyth *(Martyn Read)*

PCA   2-Axle Alumina Tank

Alcan

Number range / Notes

ALCN 11200 - 11243
Built 1975 by BREL Doncaster
Converted 2001 by E. G. Steele

BAHS 55531 - 55573
Built 1988 by Powell Duffryn

Specific Flows

Alumina :
North Blyth to Lynemouth
North Blyth to Fort William

PCA	Built	: (See text)
No. BAHS 55561	Location	: Tyne Yard *(Ken Short)*

PDA   2-Axle Van

Number range

MODA 7451 - 7473

Notes

Converted from redundant VCA vans.

Flows

MoD traffic

PDA	Built	: 1973 - 1985 by Procor	
No. MODA 7472	Location	: Didcot Parkway	*(Brian Daniels)*

PFA   2-Axle Container Flat

Number range

DRSL 92703 - BFL 92856

Specific flows

DRSL coded wagons:
Low Level Waste :
Sellafield to Drigg

BFL coded wagons:
Chemicals :
Doncaster to Mossend
(via *Enterprise*)

PFA	Built	: 1986 - 1988 by Standard Wagon	
No. DRSL 92723	Location	: Carlisle Kingmoor	*(David Kirwin)*

PFA   2-Axle Container Flat

Number range

MODA 93203 - 93238

Flows

MoD traffic

PFA	Built	: 1987 by Procor	
No. MODA 93211	Location	: Didcot Parkway	*(Martin Buck)*

PFA   **Bogie Container Wagon**

Number range : SRL 95490 / SRL 95491

Notes   : The 'Drain Train' - unusually coded in the 2-axle PFA range.

Flows   : Infrastructure work.

| PFA | Built | : 1974 - 1976 by BREL Ashford | |
| No. SRL 95490 | Location | : Rugby | *(Martyn Read)* |

| PFA | Built | : 1974 - 1976 by BREL Ashford | |
| No. SRL 95491 | Location | : Rugby | *(Martyn Read)* |

PGA   2-Axle Stone Hopper

Number range

Mendip Rail

PR   14176 - 14197

(ex-Foster Yeoman hoppers)

VTG   14203 - 14263

VTG   14378 - 14461

VTG   14747

(ex-ARC hoppers)

Notes

These former ARC and Yeoman wagons come in a variety of designs and liveries.

Typical flows

Sand :

Dagenham to :

Acton / Brentford Theale

West Drayton

Marks Tey to Crawley

Stone :

Appleford to :

Ardingly / West Drayton

PGA Build Details:

Number range:

PR 14176 to PR 14197

1989 by Procor

PR / VTG 14203 to 14263

1972 - 1974 by Chas Roberts

PR / VTG 14265 to 14461

1979 to 1981 by Procor

**All photographs
by Martin Buck**

| PGA | Built | : (See text) |
| No. PR 14188 | Location | : Acton Mainline |

| PGA | Built | : (See text) |
| No. VTG 14747 | Location | : Acton Mainline |

| PGA | Built | : (See text) |
| No. VTG 14213 | Location | : Wool Sand terminal |

| PGA | | Built | : 1977 - 1986 by Procor and Standard Wagon |
| Nos. REDA 14797 & 14513 | | Location | : Wellingborough |

(Martin Buck)

| PGA | Built | : 1977 - 1986 by Procor and Standard Wagon |
| No. REDA 14766 | Location | : Wellingborough |

(Martin Buck)

PGA   2-Axle Stone Hopper

Number range

VTG 14346 - 14377

Notes

VTG wagon on hire to EWS. Illustration, page 170.

Typical flows

Stone :
Bardon Hill to Watford

Sand:
Dagenham to Bow
Wool to Watford

PGA   2-Axle Stone Hopper   *Lafarge*

Number range

REDA 14500 - 14522

REDA 14750 - 14839

Specific flows

Stone :
From Mountsorrel to receiving terminals, including:
Barham / Broxbourne / Elstow / Kennett / Trowse / Radlett

PHA   Self-Discharge Train   *Lafarge*

Number ranges

REDA 16000 - 16081 (PHA - P)
REDA 16100 - 16103 (PHA - Q)
REDA 16200 - 16223 (PHA - R)
REDA 16300 - 16309 (PHA - S)

Notes

To enable Lafarge to supply stone to locations where no discharge facilities exist, a unique set of trains were designed, consisting of four types of hopper wagons linked by an on-board conveyor belt, which feeds a discharge wagon (KJA) built from an old container flat:

PHA - P : Basic Hopper

PHA - Q : Basic Hopper with Generator

PHA - R : Basic Hopper fitted with belt tensioner

PHA - S : Basic Hopper generator

Built 1988 - 1989 by Standard Wagon.

Illustrations, page 166 and 167.

Typical flows

Stone   :

From Mountsorrel to many locations, such as:
Banbury / Boston / Broxbourne / Chesterton Junction / Northampton / Small Heath.

PHA - P   No. 16011

PHA - Q   No. 16101

PHA - R No. 16201

PHA - S No. 16302

All photographs taken at Rugby by Martin Buck

PJA Bogie 'Comtic' 4-unit Articulated Open Van Carrier

Number range

STVA 90012 - 90015   STVA 90024 - 90027   STVA 90048 - 90051

Notes

Although these wagons operate in fixed, four unit formations, each of the four sections is individually numbered.

Unusually coded in the 'P' prefix 2-axle range.

Illustration, page 171.

Typical flows

Automotive :

Ford traffic from Dagenham and Southampton

PNA   2-Axle Box Wagon

Number range

CAIB 3600-3849

Flows

Engineers trains

| PNA | Built | : Converted 1998 - 1999 by Marcroft | |
| No. CAIB 3817 | Location | : Parkeston Quay | (Martin Buck) |

PNA   2-Axle Open Wagon   *Plasmor*

Number range

PLAS 4669 - 4694

PLAS 5269 - 5446

Specific flows

Concrete Blocks :

Heck to Biggleswade and Bow.

PNA	**Built**	: 1977 - 1979 by BREL Shildon
No. PLAS 4670	**Location**	: Peterborough

(Ian Delgado)

PNA	**Built**	: 1989 by W H Davis
No. PLAS 5271	**Location**	: Doncaster

(John Skipsey)

PGA   Built : 1980 by Procor   No. VTG 14348   Swindon Transfer Sidings   *(Martin Buck)*

PJA   Built : 1966 - 1967 by Rootes Pressings   No. STVA 90015   Eastleigh   *(Brian Daniels)*

RRA / RRB   **2-Axle Runner**

Number range

OBA conversions
110532 - 110790

VDA conversions
200777 / 200852 / 210128 / 210135 / 210137

FPA conversions
400001 - 400277

Notes

Original wagons built between 1970 and 1979 at BREL Ashford and Shildon.

Converted as runners for use with BDA / BEAs on steel trains, any excess length of steel overhanging the RRA wagon.

Specific flows

Spacers on Steel trains :
Lackenby / Scunthorpe to
Bristol East Depot and Mostyn

| RRA | No. 110764 | Newport | (Martin Buck) |

RRA   No. 200777   Doncaster   (Martyn Read)

RRB   No. 400018   Newport   (Martin Buck)

SDA / SEA / SPA   2-Axle Open Plate Wagon

Number range   : 460005 - 461100

Notes   : These wagons carry coil, rod, plate, tube and wire.

     The SPA is fitted with bolsters.

Typical flows   **EWS**

Steel :   Cardiff Tidal to Rotherham

         Sheerness to Rotherham   (via *Enterprise*)

         Aldwarke to Tees Dock

Network Rail (SPAs)

Infrastructure services

SSA   2-Axle Open Scrap Wagon

Number range   : 470000 - 470180

Notes   : Illustration, page 176.

Typical flows   : Scrap Metal -   Handsworth / Shipley / Stockton to Aldwarke

                 St. Blazey to Cardiff Tidal

SDA	Built	: 1979 - 1981 by BREL Ashford / Shildon	
No. 460775	Location	: Tees Yard	*(Martyn Read)*

SEA	Built	: 1979 - 1981 by BREL Ashford / Shildon	
No. 460966	Location	: Grangetown	*(Martyn Read)*

SPA
No. 460049

Built : 1979 - 1981 by BREL Ashford / Shildon
Location : Hoo Junction

(Mike Cubberley)

SPA
No. 460850

Built : 1979 - 1981 by BREL Ashford / Shildon
Location : Thornaby

(Martin Buck)

SSA   Built : 1982 - 1984 by Standard Wagon   No. 470020   Warrington Yard   *(Martin Buck)*

TUA   Built : 1981 by CFPM   No. NACO 74023   Parkeston Quay   *(Martin Buck)*

TDA   90 ton Bogie Petroleum Tank Wagon

Lindsey traffic:

Number range

TIPH 78200 - 78277   (excluding 78253 - 78262)

CAIB 86910 - 86969

Notes

Nos. 86910 - 86931 and 86963 - 86969 in the CAIB range are Avgas)

Typical flows

Petroleum Products :
Lindsey to Theale / Westerleigh
Humber to Bedworth

Aviation Fuel :
Lindsey to Colnbrook

Robeston traffic : Murco

Number range

TIPH 78253 - 78262 and 78278   (VTG ex Tiphook)

Specific flows

Petroleum Products :
Robeston to Theale / Westerleigh

TDA	**Built**	: 1993 by Bombardier Prorail
No. CAIB 86924	**Location**	: Didcot Parkway

(Richard Jones)

| TDA | Built | : 1990 by Marley Industrial | |
| No. TIPH 78204 | Location | : Washwood Heath | *(Martin Buck)* |

| TDA | Built | : 1990 by Marley Industrial | |
| No. TIPH 78258 | Location | : Swindon | *(Martin Buck)* |

TEA   Built : 1979 - 1981 by BREL Ashford / Shildon   No. BPO 80562   Tyne Yard   *(Ken Short)*

TEA   Built : 2006 by Wagony Swidnica, Poland   No. VTG 88130   Swindon   *(Martin Buck)*

TEA 100 ton Bogie Petroleum Tank Wagon *BP*

Number range : BPO 80160 - 80576

Notes : There are 12 in traffic, plus two wagons (VTG 80163 + VTG 80167) which work the Welton - Immingham crude oil flow.

Illustration, page 180.

Specific flows : Petroleum - Grangemouth to Dalston / Riccarton

Avgas - Grangemouth to Sinfin (via *Enterprise*)

TEA 100 ton Bogie Petroleum Tank Wagon *Total*

Number range : VTG 82200 - 82227

Typical flows : Fuel Oil - Lindsey to various power stations

Heating Oil - Lindsey to Kingsbury / Jarrow / Rectory Junction

TEA 100 ton Bogie Tank Wagon *Bitumen traffic*

Number range : CAIB / VTG 82500 - 82523

Notes : Illustration, page 185.

Specific flows : Bitumen - Lindsey to Preston Dock

TEA 100 ton Bogie Petroleum Tank Wagon *Procor*

Number range : PR 82730 - 82746

PR 82748 - 82773

Notes : The ex-Procor tank wagons in the PR 82730 - 82746 range are 'Pot-Bellied'.

Illustrations, page 184.

Flows : The 'Pot Bellied' tanks are mainly used for Gas Oil traffic from Lindsey to Neville Hill, while the conventional tanks find work on general petroleum traffic to various terminals in the UK.

TEA 100 ton Bogie Petroleum Tank Wagon *Total*

Number range : VTG 83095 - 83793

Notes : These are 'classic' bogie petroleum tank wagons, dating back to the 1960s.

Illustration, page 185.

Flows : Fuel Oil - Lindsey to various power stations

Heating Oil - Lindsey to Kingsbury / Jarrow / Rectory Junction

Bitumen - Lindsey to Preston Dock.

TEA   Built : 1980 by Standard Wagon   No. VTG 82201   Jarrow   *(Martyn Read)*

TEA	Built	: 1978 by Procor	
No. PR 82739	Location	: Kingsbury, West Midlands	*(Martin Buck)*

TEA	Built	: 1981 - 1986 by Procor	
No. PR 82762	Location	: Barnetby Chase	*(Dave Skipsey)*

TEA
No. CAIB 82513

Built : 1986 - 1987 by C C Crump
Location : Preston Docks

(John Cottrell)

TEA
No. VTG 83095

Built : 1967 - 1972 by Metro-Cammell and Chas Roberts
Location : Bescot

(Ian Delgado)

TEA   100 ton Bogie Petroleum Tank Wagon   *BRT*

Number range

BRT 84060   BRT 84080 - 84089   (all remaining vehicles are TEBs)

Specific flows

Avgas :
Lindsey to Colnbrook

Crude Oil :
Welton to Immingham

TEA   100 ton Bogie Petroleum Tank Wagon   *Murco*

Number range

PR 85300 - 85316 (VTG ex-Procor)

Specific flows

Petroleum :
Robeston to Theale / Westerleigh

TEA   100 ton Bogie Petroleum Tank Wagon

Number range

VTG 85945 - 85974

Typical flows

Petroleum Products :
Lindsey to Kingsbury / Jarrow / Rectory Junction

TEA	**Built** : 1968 - 1972 by Chas Roberts, MetroCammell and Pickering
No. BRT 84081	**Location** : Harrowden Junction, Wellingborough *(Graham Lee)*

TEA
No. PR 85300

Built : 1981 by Procor
Location : Swindon

(Martin Buck)

TEA
No. VTG 85966

Built : 1988 by Standard Wagon
Location : York

(Martyn Read)

TEA   100 ton Bogie Petroleum Tank Wagon

Number range

BPO / CAIB / VTG 87105 - 87971

Notes

These 'classic' bogie petroleum tank wagons date back to the 1960's.

Built between 1967 and 1972 by Chas Roberts, Metro-Cammell, Pickering and Powell Duffryn.

The Holybourne and Welton flows of crude oil use only 22 and 14 tank wagons, respectively.

Typical flows

Petroleum :
Grangemouth to Dalston / Riccarton

Avgas :
Grangemouth to Sinfin (via *Enterprise*)

Crude Oil :
Fawley to Holybourne
Welton to Immingham

TEA   No. BPO 87880   Location : Greenhill Lower Junction   *(Dave Skipsey)*

Opposite : TEA vehicles in the consist of 6Y33, Holybourne - Eastleigh, at Eastleigh.   *(Martin Buck)*

TEA No. VTG 87486

TEA No. VTG 87878

TEA No. VTG 87887

TEA   100 ton Bogie Fuel Oil Tank Wagon   *Caib / VTG*

Number range / Specific flows   *(Carless)*

CAIB 88001 - 88020

Condensate :
North Walsham to Harwich

Number range / Flows   *(Conoco)*   Illustration, page 192.

CAIB 88021 - 88080

Petroleum :
Humber to Kingsbury and Jarrow

Number range / Specific flows

CAIB 88081 - 88093

Styrene :
Immingham to Stalybridge

Notes

Similar in appearance to TEAs on the North Walsham flow, but without any branding.

The loaded Styrene tanks run overnight and the empties return late evening, making it difficult to obtain illustrations of these particular TEAs.

Number range / Specific flows   *(Petroplus)*   Illustration, page 192.

VTG 88094 - 88114

Petroleum :
Port Clarence to Bedworth / Westerleigh

Number range / Specific flows   *(Murco)*   Illustration, page 181.

VTG 88115 - 88137

Petroleum :
Robeston to Theale / Westerleigh

Notes

Introduced in 2006 to replace older TEAs on the Robeston circuit.

Number range / Typical flows   Illustrations, page 193.

VTG 88143 - 88174

Petroleum :
Humber to Kingsbury / Jarrow

TEA Built : 2001 by Marcroft No. CAIB 88008 Parkeston Quay *(Martin Buck)*

TEA	Built	: 2001 by Marcroft	
No. CAIB 88054	Location	: Kingsbury	*(Martin Buck)*

TEA	Built	: 2001 by Marcroft	
No. VTG 88113	Location	: Milford Junction	*(John Skipsey)*

TEA   Built   : 2006 by Wagony Swidnica, Poland
No. VTG 88144   Location   : Kingsbury   *(Martin Buck)*

TEA   Built   : 2006 by Wagony Swidnica, Poland
No. VTG 88172   Location   : Barnetby   *(Martin Buck)*

T   2-Axle & Bogie Petrochemical Tank Wagons

TEA   100 ton Bogie Tank Wagon   *GERS*

Number range : GERS 89001 - 89028 (GE Rail Services)

Specific flows : Petroleum - Robeston to Theale / Westerleigh

TEA   Bogie Tank Wagon   *Calcium Carbonate*

Number range : NACO 89100 - 89129

Specific flows : Calcium Carbonate - Quidhampton to Workington

TEA   *EWS* 100 ton Bogie Petroleum Tank Wagon

Number range : EWS 870200 - 870344

Notes : Introduced in 2006 to replace older TEAs on the Lindsey circuit.
Illustration, page 196.

Typical flows : Petroleum   - Lindsey to:
Products   Jarrow / Kingsbury / Rectory Junction / Theale / Westerleigh

Aviation Fuel   - Lindsey to Colnbrook
Fuel Oil   - Lindsey to Aberthaw / Didcot / Drax / Eggborough / Ferrybridge
Ironbridge / Rugeley / West Burton power stations

TEA   *FHH* 100 ton Bogie Petroleum Tank Wagon

Number range : FLHH 871001 - 871006

Notes : Illustration, page 196.

Typical flows : Petroleum - Humber to Kingsbury and Jarrow

TIA   100 ton Internationally Registered Bogie Tank Wagon

Number range : 33. 70. 7899. 001 to 060

Notes : These are the only 100-ton bogie petroleum tanks working out of Humber and
Lindsey refineries to be classified in the RIV wagon series.
Illustrations, page 197.

Specific flows : Petroleum - Humber to Bedworth
Lindsey to Westerleigh

Number range : 33. 70. 7899. 022 to 038

Specific flows : Nitric Acid - Middlesbrough to Sellafield

TEA
No. GERS 89010

Built   : 2001 by Arbel Fauvet, France
Location : Swindon

(Martin Buck)

TEA
No. NACO 89114

Built   : 2003 by Wagony Swidnica, Poland
Location : Eastleigh

(Martin Buck)

TEA	Built	: 2006 by Wagony Swidnica, Poland	
No. EWS 870217	Location	: Washwood Heath	*(Martin Buck)*

TEA	Built	: 2006 by Wagony Swidnica, Poland	
No. FLHH 871002	Location	: Barnetby	*(Martin Buck)*

TIA

No. 33. 70. 7899. 049

Built : 1987 by Arbel Fauvet, France

Location : Water Orton

(Mark Franklin)

TIA

No. 33. 70. 7899. 034

Built : 1987 by Arbel Fauvet, France

Location : Healey Mills

(Martyn Read)

TTA	Built	: (See text)	
No. BPO 53754	Location	: Coatbridge Central	*(Alexander Clark)*

TTA   2-Axle Fuel Oil Tank

Grangemouth Traffic

Number range

BPO 37263

BPO 53722 - 53774

BPO 60197

BPO 60560 - 60884

Typical Flows

Aviation Fuel :
Grangemouth to :
Linkswood
Prestwick

Oil :
Grangemouth to
Lairg / Fort William

TTA	Built	: (See text)	
No. BPO 60771	Location	: Greenhill Lower	*(Dave Skipsey)*

TTA Build Details:

Number range:
BPO 37263
BPO 53722 - 53774
1965 - 1967 by
Chas Roberts and Pickering

ESSO 56001 - 56280
ESSO 61200 - 61550
ESSO 61700 - 61953

BPO   60197 - 60884
BPO   61560 - 61691

1965 - 1979 by
Chas Roberts
Metro-Cammell
Pickering
Powell Duffryn

BRT 57194 - 57231
1965 by Pressed Steel

PR 58246 - 58269
1966 by Powell Duffryn

TTA	Built	: (See text)	
No. ESSO 56208	Location	: Ipswich	*(Martin Buck)*

TTA   2-Axle Fuel Oil Tank

Number range / Typical flows

Fawley Traffic

ESSO 56001 - 56279

Fuel Oil :

Fawley to :

Bristol / Ipswich / Laira / Penzance
South Wales / St Blazey

Lindsey Traffic

BRT 57194 - 57231

PR 58246 - 58269

Fuel Oil :

Lindsey to :

Bescot / Neville Hill / Peak Forest
Thornaby / Toton / Warrington

TTA	Built	: (See text)	
No. BRT 57205	Location	: Doncaster	*(Martyn Read)*

TTA   2-Axle Bitumen Tank

Number range / Typical flows

Fawley Traffic

ESSO 61200 - 61550

ESSO 61700 - 61953

Bitumen :

Fawley to :

Bromford Bridge (Birmingham)
Cattewater (Plymouth)

Thameshaven Traffic

BPO 61560 - 61691

Bitumen :

Thameshaven to Llandarcy

TTA	Built	: (See text)	
No. PR 58256	Location	: Warringon Yard	*(Martin Buck)*

TTA	Built	: (See text)	
No. ESSO 61909	Location	: Bromford Bridge	*(Martin Buck)*

TUA   2-Axle Fuel Oil Tank

Number range   :   PR 70048 - 70117   NACO 74001 - 74029

Notes   :   Built 1965 - 1981 by Chas Roberts, CFPM, Pickering, Standard Wagon

Typical flows   :   Fuel Oil : Lindsey to Bescot / Neville Hill / Peak Forest / Thornaby / Toton

Mud Oil - Harwich to Aberdeen   (*Carless* - Illustration, page 177)

TUA	Built	: (See text)	
No. PR 70065	Location	: Warrington Yard	*(Martin Buck)*

TUA	Built	: (See text)	
No. NACO 74006	Location	: Doncaster	*(Martin Buck)*

VGA / VKA   2-Axle Van

Number range : 210402 - 210650

Typical flows : MoD Traffic - MoD Stores around the UK
Paper   - Immingham to Ely / Deanside
Zinc :   - Immingham to Bloxwich

| VGA | Built | : 1983 by BREL, Shildon | |
| No. 210474 | Location | : Didcot Yard | *(Martin Buck)* |

| VKA | Built | : 1983 by BREL, Shildon | |
| No. 210648 | Location | : Eastleigh | *(Martin Buck)* |

WIA   Enclosed Car Transporter

Number range

(85) 70. 4971. 000 to 059

Notes

An impressive light blue liveried 5-unit, articulated, enclosed car carrier, where the anti-vandal covers are lifted out of the way in order to load / unload the wagons.

Typical flows

Automotive :

Minis   : Cowley (Oxford) to Purfleet

Jaguars : Halewood (Liverpool) / Castle Bromwich (Birmingham) to Southampton

Hondas : South Marston (Swindon) to Dollands Moor

WIA	Built	: 1995 by Arbel Fauvet, France	
No. 85. 70. 4971. 059	Location	: Washwood Heath	*(Martin Buck)*

Opposite :

Class 92 No. 92022 *Charles Dickens* slowly makes her way out of Kingmoor Yard, Carlisle, with the 17:23 hrs 'Enterprise' service bound for Eastleigh; very reminiscent of former 'Speedlink' days! The consist includes empty calcium carbonate ICA bogie tanks (for Quidhampton), MoD containers (Didcot), JNAs of scrap metal (Bescot) and empty limestone JAA / JIA covered hoppers (Warrington).

(Martin Buck)

Glossary

Carkinds Removed

During the compilation of 'Wagon Recognition', some 'Carkinds' were taken out of revenue earning traffic, stored or withdrawn altogether.

These wagon types, whilst not included in the main section of this book, are detailed below along with an image of each for completeness.

Carkind	Description	Number Range
CSA	Fly Ash Presflo Wagon	876057 - 876064
CTA	Bogie Brine Tank Wagon	870000 - 870015
FFA	Freightliner Inner Wagon	602090 - 603248
FGA	Freightliner Outer Wagon	601026 - 601842
FPA	2-Axle Container Wagon	400001 - 400295
HDA	2-Axle MGR Coal Hopper	368000 - 368459
JIA	Bogie Starch Tank	(33) 70. 9292. 200 - 214
JIA	Covered Bogie China Clay Hopper	(33) 70. 9382. 000 - 129
KAA*	Bogie Mega 3 Wagon	BCC 11501 - 11522
KFA	BNFL Bogie Container Wagon	BNFL 95474 / 75 / 84
MKA	2-Axle Open Box Wagon	390150 - 390331
		393000 - 393035
OTA	Timber Carrier	112000 - 112398
		200552 - 200997
PKA	3-Axle 'Donelli Carrier'	RLS 92338 / 339 / 342 / 343
TEA	100 Ton Hydrochloric Acid Tank	WHD 83901 - 83907

* The KAAs have been sold by Lafarge to Nacco, for use on the continent, and are now IXAs, numbered in the 37.80.4905.xxx series.

CSA   Converted : 1999 - 2000 by Procor   No. 876064   Peak Forest   *(Gareth Bayer)*

CTA   Converted : 2005 by Marcroft   No. 87007   Warrington Yard   *(Dave Skipsey)*

FPA   Built : 1970 - 1971 by BREL Ashford   No. 400162   Newport

(Martyn Read)

FFA   Built : 1966 - 1973 by BREL Ashford / Shildon   No. 603182   Rugby   *(Martyn Read)*

FGA   Built : 1966 - 1976 by BREL Ashford / Shildon   No. 601167   Rugby   *(Martyn Read)*

HDA   Built : 1980 - 1982 by BREL Shildon   No. 368048   Newport   *(Martin Buck)*

JIA   Built : 1983 by Standard Wagon   No. 33. 70. 9382. 081   Par   *(Martyn Read)*

JIA   Built : 1987 by Arbel Fauvet, France   No. 33. 70. 9292. 201   Tavistock Junction, Plymouth   *(Allan Wright)*

KAA   Built : 2002 - 2003 by Babcock Rail   No. BCC 115xx series   Oakley, Bedford   *(Nigel Gibbs)*

KFA
Built : 1983 by Standard Wagon
No. BNFL 95 Series
Seascale
(Dave McAlone)

MKA   Converted : 1993 - 1994 at York WRD / Carlisle Currock   No. 390318   Didcot Yard   *(Martin Buck)*

OTA   Built : 1975 - 1982 by BREL Shildon   No. 210129   Brandon   *(Gareth Bayer)*

PKA   Built : 1981 - 1983 by Societe Nouvelle des Ateliers / Fauvet Girel, France

No. RLS 92332 & RLS 92333   Hitchin

(Gareth Bayer)

TEA   **Built : 1967 - 1969 by W H Davis**   No. WHD 83903   Warrington Bank Quay   *(Peter Cummings)*

WAGON 'HOTSPOTS'

There are many 'Wagon Hotspots' around the country ideal for observing freight traffic and studying Carkinds at close quarters. Some are better than others and here is a guide on the best locations to visit for specific Carkinds, based upon commodity - coal, metals, etc:

Commodity / Location(s)	Carkinds
Aggregate	
Peak Forest	HOA / JGA / JHA / JMA / MBA / MJA
Acton	HLA / HOA / JGA / JHA / KEA / MBA / MJA / PGA
Westbury	JFA / JGA / JHA / JNA / JYA / KEA / MJA
Automotive	
Washwood Heath	IFA / IGA / IPA / WIA
Coal	
Barnetby / Carlisle	HAA / HHA / HMA / HTA / HXA / MEA
Knottingley	HAA / HHA / HMA / HTA / HXA / HYA
Enterprise	
Rugby / Warrington	ICA / IMA / IVA / IWA / IZA / KVA / VGA
Intermodal	
Eastleigh	FAA / FCA / FEA / FIA / FKA / FLA / FSA / FTA / KFA / KTA
Rugby	As above, plus IKA / KSA
Metals	
Newport	BAA / BBA / BCA / BDA / BEA / BFA / BLA / BRA / BYA IHA / KIA / JSA / RRA / SEA / SPA / SSA
Doncaster	As for Newport, plus BIA / BWA / BXA / BWA / FIA
Tees Yard	As Newport, plus BMA / BNA / BPA / BSA / BTA / BZA / IFB / SDA
Minerals (Limestone)	
Peak Forest	HIA / JAA / JEA / JGA / JIA / MBA / MEA
Tees Yard	CBA / HCA / HFA / HGA / HNA / JGA
MoD	
Didcot	KFA / KWA / PDA / PFA / VGA / VKA
Petroleum Products	
Barnetby	TDA / TEA / TIA / TTA / TUA

Please note that other Carkinds can also be seen at the above locations.

SPECIAL CARKINDS

In addition to the Carkinds listed under 'Wagon Hotspots', there are other Carkinds which only work specific routes / areas of the country; here is a guide of suggested locations on where to see them.

Carkind	Description	Commodity	Location
BVA	Bogie Steel Flat Wagon	Steel	Barnetby
CDA	2-Axle China Clay Hopper	China Clay	Par
FBA	*EWS* Bogie Flat	Gypsum	Doncaster
FNA	*DRS* Flatrol Atomic Flask wagon	Flasks	Sellafield
FPA	2-Axle Container Wagon	Gypsum	Doncaster
HEA	2-Axle Domestic Coal Hopper	Coke	Tees Yard
IFA	Long Welded Rail wagon	Rails	Eastleigh
IFA	2-Axle Container Flat	Ford 'Blue Train'	Stratford
IGA	Bogie Flat	Rails	Eastleigh
INA	Articulated Bogie Twin	Automotive	Stratford
IRB	Covered Hopper	Silica Sand	Newport
JGA	Bogie Cement Wagon	Cement	Peak Forest
JGA	Bogie Covered Hopper	Potash	Grangetown
JGA	*Bardon* Bogie Aggregate Hopper	Stone	Bedford
JGA	*Tarmac* Bogie Covered Hopper	Stone	Leeds
JIA	Bogie Covered Hopper	Potash	Grangetown
JIA	Bogie Covered Hopper	China Clay	Par
JNA	Bogie Scrap wagon	Scrap Metal	Willesden Junction
JPA	Bogie Cement Wagon	Cement	Chesterfield
JRA	*Bardon* Bogie Agrregate Hopper	Stone	Bedford
JTA	Bogie Tippler - Outer	Iron ore	Barnetby
JUA	Bogie Tippler - Inner	Iron Ore	Barnetby
JXA	Bogie Scrap Wagon	Scrap Metal	Warrington
JZA	Bogie Long Welded Rail Carrier	Rails	Doncaster
KFA	Bogie Open Sided Carrier	Timber	Warrington
KJA	Bogie Unloading wagon (use on Lafarge Self Discharge Train)	Aggregate	Nuneaton
KUA	Bogie Nuclear Flask Transporter	Flasks	Sellafield
KXA	Bogie Nuclear Flask Transporter	Flasks	Sellafield
KYA	Bogie Nuclear Flask Transporter	Flasks	Sellafield
OAA	2-Axle Open Sided Wagon	Concrete Blocks	Westbury
PAA	2-Axle Sand Hopper	Sand	Peterborough
PCA	2-Axle Alumina Tank	Alumina	Tyne Yard
PCA	2-Axle Cement Tank	Cement	Bedford
PFA	2-Axle Container Flat	Low level Waste	Sellafield
PGA	*Lafarge* 2-Axle Stone Hopper	Stone	Bedford
PHA	Self-Discharge Train	Stone	Nuneaton
PJA	Bogie 'Comtic' 4-Unit Van Carrier	Vans	Eastleigh
PNA	*Plasmor* 2-Axle Open Wagon	Concrete Blocks	Peterborough
TEA	Bogie Tank Wagon	Calcium Carbonate	Eastleigh

INFRASTRUCTURE 'CARKINDS'

Infrastructure and engineers trains work throughout the UK rail network, employing a variety of Carkinds; here is a summary of Carkinds which can be deployed:

For example:

EWS

FDA	Twin Container Flat	621454 - 621542
FJA	Bogie Flat Wagon	621900 - 621917
FZA	Bogie Rail Wagon	600500 - 600502
MCA	Bogie Low Sided Open Box Wagon	500201 - 500240
MDA	Bogie Low Sided Open Box Wagon	500241 - 500300
MFA	2-Axle Low Sided Open Box Wagon	391001 - 391617
MHA	2-Axle Low Sided Open Box Wagon	394001 - 396165
MLA	Bogie Low Sided Open Ballast Wagon	503501 - 503515
MOA	Bogie Low Sided Open Box Wagon	500301 - 500350
MTA	2-Axle Open Box Wagon	395001 - 395405
OBA	2-Axle Open Box Wagon	110000 - 110800
OCA	2-Axle Open Box Wagon	112000 - 112398

GBRf

FEA - S	Bogie Flat Wagon	640631 - 640693
FEA - S	Bogie Flat Wagon	640901 - 640922
HQA - K/L/M	Autoballaster	380701 - 380710
MLA	Bogie Low Sided Open Ballast Wagon	503001 - 503140

FREIGHTLINER HEAVY HAUL

FEA - E	Bogie Flat Wagon	641001 - 641066

NETWORK RAIL

FEA - S	Bogie Flat Wagon	642001 - 642050
HQA - A to J	Autoballaster	380001 - 380410
JJA	Autoballaster	GERS 12901 - GERS 13005
KRA	Bogie Sleeper Wagon	NR 97101 - NR 97132
MRA	Bogie Side Tipping Ballast Wagon	501001 - 501400
PNA	2-Axle Open Box Wagon	CAIB 3600 - CAIB 3849
SPA	2-Axle Open Plate Wagon	460005 - 461100

BALFOUR BEATTY

FEA - B	Bogie Flat Wagon	640501 - 640514
FEA - D	Bogie Flat Wagon	640571 - 640576

TRANSPLANT

FEA - S	Bogie Flat Wagon ('Slingers')	640931 - 640943

BIBLIOGRAPHY

Websites

General

Wagons On The Web	Gareth Bayer	wagons.wordpress.com
UK Rolling Stock	Martyn Read	ukrailways.fototopic.net

Wider reference

Continental Wagons	Rob Volland	uicstock.org.uk

Books

UK & Continental Wagons	AEB 27 Chatsworth Avenue Warton PRESTON PR4 1BQ	No ISBN number
Combined Wagon Datafile	Inter City Railway Society 192 Alvechurch Road West Heath Birmingham B31 3PW	No ISBN number

ACKNOWLEDGEMENTS

Images have been kindly submitted for this project by:

Tony Atkinson	Gareth Bayer	Glenn Britcliffe	Alexander Clark
John Cottrell	Mike Cubberley	Peter Cummings	Brian Daniels
Ian Delgado	S. Evans	EWS	Mark Franklin
Nigel Gibbs	Mike Honeyman	Richard Jones	Andy Jupe
Dave Kerwin	Graham Lee	Colin Marsden	Dave McAlone
Jim Ramsay	Martyn Read	Ken Short	Dave Skipsey
John Skipsey	Barrie Swann	Rob Terrace	Mick Tindall
Allan Wright			

Notes

Notes